W9-AZB-870

SURVIVAL
QUEST

Hershey Christian School
P.O. Box 378
Hershey, PA 17033

VOLUME TWO

STUDENT EDITION

Authors

SHARON R. BERRY, Ph.D., and OLLIE E. GIBBS, Ed.D.

LifeWay
CHURCH RESOURCES
Biblical Solutions for Life

CHURCH RESOURCES

Biblical Solutions for Life

Published by
LifeWay Christian School Resources
One LifeWay Plaza
Nashville, TN 37234-0182

Created and Developed by

Christian Academic Publications and Services, Inc.
Birmingham, Alabama

ISBN: 0-7673-9340-6
Dewey Decimal Classification: 248.82
Subject Heading: TEENAGERS/CHRISTIAN LIFE

No portion of this book may be reproduced in any way without the written permission of the publisher, except for brief excerpts in reviews, etc.

SurvivalQuest, Volume Two: Student Edition

© 1999, Reprint 2003, Christian Academic Publications and Services, Inc.
Printed in the United States of America
All rights reserved

SurvivalQuest

Table of Contents

Scripture quotations not otherwise marked are taken
from the *New King James Version.*
Copyright © 1982 by Thomas Nelson, Inc.
Used by permission. All rights reserved.

Scripture quotations marked (KJV) are from
The Holy Bible, King James Version.

Scripture quotations marked (NIV) are from
The Holy Bible, New International Version.
Copyright © 1978 by New York International Bible Society.
Used by permission of the Zondervan Bible Publishers.

Scripture quotations marked (NASB) are taken from
The New American Standard Bible.
Copyright © The Lockman Foundation, 1960, 1962, 1963, 1968,
1971, 1972, 1973, 1975, 1977, 1995.
Used by permission.

Scripture quotations marked (TLB) are taken from
The Living Bible
Copyright © 1971 by Tyndale House Publishers.
Used by permission. All rights reserved.

INTRODUCTION

Surviving and Thriving

Stress, hurt, anxiety, frustrations, anger, disappointments, depression, bewilderment, crisis, panic. Life is tough. And it's getting tougher for young teens. What can you do? Give up? Go hide in a cave? Sit in a corner and suck your thumb?

You are about to begin the second half of a 36-week course entitled *SurvivalQuest*. You will learn practical, down-to-earth skills based on Biblical examples and principles. Beyond surviving the upsets of life, you will learn to thrive as you develop relationships and build toward your future. Perhaps no other study could be more important to you at this time of life.

Do bad things happen to young teens? They surely do. Students at a high school in Paducah, Kentucky, found this out when a classmate opened fire on a group meeting for prayer. Ben Strong, a 17-year-old, spoke these words at his friends' funeral: "They died for what they believed in. It hurts to see them go, but to them, there was no better way. They were praying. As soon as they said, 'amen,' they saw the face of God."

A few months later a similar incident occurred in a middle school in Jonesboro, Arkansas. A 13-year-old and an 11-year-old opened fire on their classmates and teachers who had exited Westside School for a false fire alarm. After murdering four classmates and a teacher, the two have nothing to look forward to except to lie on their cots and cry for their mothers. The motivation for such devastation? The older boy's girlfriend had broken up with him.

In listening to the media coverage of these events, we share the anguish and grief of families and friends suffering the loss of loved ones. Our hearts ache for students who couldn't solve their deep emotional conflicts in more positive and productive ways. We are left with the questions: How could such a thing happen, and how can it be prevented in the future?

More quietly and with less fanfare, 1.5 million teens a year attempt suicide feeling that they have nothing to live for or that their mistakes are so grievous, they cannot face the future. Other teens turn to gangs, sex or crime seeking a way to ease their deep hurts and satisfy the longings of their hearts.

There are better ways to resolve the conflicts and hurts. Without making light of the problems you face, your study of *SurvivalQuest* will provide you with choices and solutions. You will learn to accept your natural emotions and desires as you exercise options toward recovery and growth. You will learn not only to survive, but to thrive in the midst of your circumstances.

Throughout your study you will be drawn back to the characteristics of God, who made you and loves you. Knowing He is sovereign—in control of all events and their outcomes—can give you the confidence to face tomorrow. When you feel that there is no hope, no way out of the pit, God can magnificently step into your life to bring peace and sureness of the future (Jeremiah 31:3–4; 29:11).

> *". . . Yes, I have loved you with an everlasting love; therefore with loving-kindness I have drawn you. Again I will build you . . . . For I know the thoughts that I think toward you . . . thoughts of peace and not of evil, to give you a future and a hope."*

Nobody messes up too much for God. No one is beyond His power to forgive and restore. Having extensively persecuted early Christian believers and assented to the death of Stephen, the Apostle Paul called himself the worst of sinners. Arrogant, prideful, self-centered and self-sufficient, Paul was a wreck, yet God could bring victory and joy to his life. After becoming a believer, Paul's life was no flower garden. The Christians distrusted him. The Jews hated him, stoned him and left him for dead. He suffered disappointing friendships, imprisonment, shipwreck, poor health—you name it. But in the end, Paul wrote the song of the overcomer (Romans 8:28, 31–32, 37).

"And we know that all things work together for good to those who love God, to those who are the called according to His purpose . . . . If God is for us, who can be against us? He who did not spare his own Son, but delivered Him up for us all, how shall He not with Him also freely give us all things? Yet in all these things we are more than conquerors through Him who loved us."

We can overcome. We can survive. And we can thrive. But to do so, we must follow the same foundational steps as Paul. As you read each step, consider whether you have honestly taken this step in your own life. God's way or no way, the choice is yours.

1. Recognize God as the source of all goodness and happiness in this life and the life to come. With Him, all things are possible. Without Him, nothing is. Because He is life, light and love, He alone has the wisdom to provide clear direction for your life, the power to help and the love to forgive.

2. Realize your own helplessness. We are made of clay and a few trace minerals. We have a mindset that is in opposition to God. The Bible says that we have deceitful hearts, determined to wickedness. Given our best efforts and best intents, we fall miserably short of God's standard. This failure is called sin. The solution is to agree that, in ourselves, we have no answers. Therefore, we come to God in confession of sin and the helpless condition of our lives.

3. Receive Christ as Savior. God's method of forgiving sin and establishing a right relationship with Him is through His Son, Jesus Christ. By faith, we accept God's provision and make a commitment to live as He commands. In return, God sends the Holy Spirit to eternally live within us, giving us the desire and ability to live as God wants.

4. Reflect the relationship you have with God. Commit to learning all you can about God through Bible reading, prayer and interaction with other believers. Apply what you learn to the everyday experiences of life. Trust that in every situation, God is in control. His plan is bigger than we can see. It ultimately leads to building our character and conforming us to be more like Christ.

5. Rejoice in all things. Because God has a purpose and the final outcome is certain, you don't have to sweat the small stuff. Even in the most difficult trials and embarrassing mistakes, you can experience hope, peace and joy. Every circumstance can be your teacher toward spiritual maturity and successful living. Embrace life with enthusiasm as you grow up in Him.

These five steps can set the course of your life. They can make you emotionally secure and confident as you face the challenges of the future. They give you what psychologists call "resilience." This is the ability to rebound from life's upsets. It is the ability to regain composure in the midst of turmoil. It is the ability to rebuild after the most devastating blows imaginable. It is a key factor in "emotional intelligence" or an EQ that is recognized as being of far greater importance than IQ, intelligence, when considering success in life.

Begin with these five steps firmly established as your goals for life. Then as you study a different Bible person each week, along with the challenges they survived, apply the principles to the various ups and downs you face. When you complete the course, you will have learned how to both survive and thrive at life. You will be an overcomer.

> ". . . they shall walk with Me in white, for they are worthy. He who overcomes shall be clothed in white garments, and I will not blot out his name from the Book of Life; but I will confess his name before My Father and before His angels." (Revelation 3:4–5)

INQUIRY-ACTION I.1

SURVEY ON CHALLENGES AND CONCERNS

ITEM	RANKING OF CONCERN		
	EXTREMELY HIGH		**LITTLE OR NONE**
	10 9 8 7 6 5 4 3 2 1 0		
	10 9 8 7 6 5 4 3 2 1 0		
	10 9 8 7 6 5 4 3 2 1 0		
	10 9 8 7 6 5 4 3 2 1 0		
	10 9 8 7 6 5 4 3 2 1 0		
	10 9 8 7 6 5 4 3 2 1 0		
	10 9 8 7 6 5 4 3 2 1 0		
	10 9 8 7 6 5 4 3 2 1 0		
	10 9 8 7 6 5 4 3 2 1 0		
	10 9 8 7 6 5 4 3 2 1 0		

INQUIRY-ACTION I.1 (CONTINUED)

LETTER TO MYSELF

Based on the personal challenges and concerns I face, some things I would like to learn in this course are:

_____

_____

_____

In order to really learn and apply Biblical solutions to life problems, I make the following promises to God and myself.

☐ I promise to work on my relationship with God.

☐ I promise to study Biblical principles and apply them to my life.

☐ I promise to pray and be sensitive to the Holy Spirit working in me.

☐ I promise to seek godly counsel when I am in situations that seem overwhelming.

☐ I promise to help others find godly solutions to the problems they face.

Signature: _____

Date: _____

INQUIRY–ACTION I.2

ROMANS 8

1. Throughout the passage we see a dramatic contrast in trying to live the human way versus living by God's Spirit. In the two columns below write words from the passage that describe these two ways to live.

The Human Way	The Way of God's Spirit

2. Based on your descriptions, which way of thinking would be best if you were facing a serious crisis? Why? _____

_____

3. Check verses 1 and 9 and explain how a person can change from a natural way of thinking to a spiritual way of thinking. _____

_____

4. Check verse 15. The term "Abba, Father" is very intimate and endearing. It's the picture of a little child who has climbed onto his dad's lap, given him a big hug and said, "You're my sweet papa." As an adopted child of God, what special protections and privileges do you have? Name at least three based on the passage.

_____

_____

_____

INQUIRY–ACTION I.2 (CONTINUED)

5. Check verse 28. God has a big plan and can see the end from the beginning. Some things that seem so bad now turn out to be a blessing later. In hindsight, you can see how God was protecting you or working things to your eventual good. Write one example of this from your personal experience.

_____

_____

6. Check verses 35 through 39. Paul wrote a long list of things that cannot separate us from God, then said, ". . . nor any other creature/created thing." Think about the challenges or problems students face. Can any separate you from God? Why or why not?

_____

_____

7. Check verse 37. Being more than a conqueror is an interesting idea. If you win, you are a conqueror. But how can you be **more** than a conqueror? Write at least two sentences to explain your ideas.

_____

_____

_____

8. Below are five principles based on Romans 8. Write the numerals 1 through 5 in the circles next to them to show their order in the Scripture.

◯ Tough times don't have to over-whelm us. We can overcome them through His love and power.

◯ Even in tough times, God has a purpose and a plan to bless us and make the eventual outcome good.

◯ Tough times cannot separate us from God's love and the future glory we will share with Him.

◯ Doing things man's way (the natural way) is opposed to doing things God's way.

◯ Christians are God's children and can be directed by His Spirit living in them.

INQUIRY-ACTION 1.3

ROMANS 8:18, 28, 31B, 35 AND 37

Use the word bank to help you write the verses from memory.

according	God	or	those
against	good	peril	through
all	glory	persecution	time
and	Him	present	to
are	His	purpose	together
be	I	revealed	tribulation
called	if	separate	us
can	in	shall	we
Christ	is	sufferings	with
compared	know	sword	which
conquerors	love	than	who
consider	loved	that	work
distress	more	the	worthy
famine	nakedness	these	yet
for	not	things	
from	of	this	

ESTHER

Surviving Position and Possessions

Billy was a bright little boy, and very competitive. Although he was only eight, he could beat almost anyone at a game of Monopoly—anyone except his grandmother! Last summer, when he spent two weeks at her house in the mountains, she beat him every time they played. It would be different this summer. He just knew it would.

As soon as he arrived at Grandma's house, he was ready to "take her on." Knowing that Billy would want to restore his reputation, she already had the Monopoly board set up. Before even unpacking his suitcase, Billy and his grandmother were challenging each other for the right to own Boardwalk. A little over two hours later, the game ended. Grandma had won again. Each day Billy and Grandma played, and each day Billy lost. When his vacation was over, Billy had failed to win even once.

Billy's grandma saw the discouragement on his face. As he was packing to go home, she shared with him, "The way to win at Monopoly is to get all of the property, houses and hotels as fast as you can." For the next year, Billy played the game of Monopoly differently. He bought property, houses and hotels as fast as he possibly could.

Summer finally came again. School was out and it was time to go to Grandma's. But more importantly, it was time for Billy to find out if all of his practice would pay off. Within a few minutes of arriving at Grandma's, the Monopoly box was opened and they were setting up the game. About three hours later, the game ended. However, the results were different this time. Billy won! Matter of fact, for the next two weeks, Billy won every game they played. He could not be stopped. He had taken his grandma's advice and beaten her at her own game.

The two weeks passed quickly. The final game of Monopoly for the summer was over and Billy had won again. With a big grin on his face, he started to leave the table. "Wait a minute," Grandma said. "You followed my advice and learned your lessons well. But it's time for you to learn another important lesson." She then picked up the Monopoly board and dumped the property, houses, hotels and money back into the box. She put the top back on and carefully tucked the Monopoly game under her arm.

"You may win the game," she said. "But never forget, I own the box!"

Grandma's lesson for Billy, and for us, is a simple one. No matter how many possessions we have and no matter how important we think we are, when the game of life is over, everything goes back into the box. In the game of life, God owns the box. Grandma's lesson for Billy illustrated the important truth of Mark 8:36, "For what will it profit a man if he gains the whole world, and loses his own soul?"

"Wanting it all and wanting it now" certainly sums up the way a lot of people think today. When it comes to possessions or achieving certain positions in life, they are determined that nothing is going to stop them from getting what they want. There seem to be fewer people who seek higher goals of service to their fellowman and to the kingdom of God—people who refuse to let possessions and position be their main focus. Esther was such a person.

The story of Esther almost reads like a modern day movie plot. It begins with a king who banishes his queen and then spends a year searching for a maiden to replace her. Among those chosen to participate in one of the first ever "Miss Kingdom Beauty Pageants" is the orphaned cousin of Mordecai. More beautiful and winsome than her peers, Esther is chosen as the new queen. Unknown to the powerful Persian king, Esther's family is Jewish, part of the captives exiled from Jerusalem during the Babylonian captivity.

The plot thickens when we learn that Haman, one of the king's chief ministers, hates Jews. He particularly hates Mordecai because of his refusal to bow and worship him. Haman tricks the king into signing a decree ordering all Jews to be executed.

Through her cousin Mordecai, Esther learns of the plot and faces a difficult decision. Should she risk her possessions and position as queen by asking the king to spare her people? Surely he would be angered at her boldness. The story has an unexpected plot twist and ending, which you can read in the book of Esther.

Esther's words, "If I perish, I perish!" prove that she was willing to sacrifice everything. As a result, her people were spared from certain destruction. Ever since that time, the Jews have celebrated their deliverance from Haman's plot and honored Esther during the religious holiday known as Purim. She also continues to be honored by descendants of the Persian people at an ancient temple built in her honor located north of the capital of Iraq.

During the perilous times Esther faced, Mordecai challenged her to consider her destiny. "Who knows whether you have come to the kingdom for such a time as this?" The same question can be asked of you. Your generation will face tremendous challenges in the world. Young people willing to sacrifice positions, possessions and even their lives are needed to serve others and the cause of Christ. You have been called for such a time as this. How will your life make a difference?

The book of Esther is unique in that it is one of only two books of the Bible that bears a woman's name. It is also unique in that God's name is never mentioned. Yet, throughout its pages the hand of God strongly directs the lives of people. Through His providence, Esther became queen and enjoyed a position of great influence and unlimited possessions. The Bible is clear that possessions and positions are not sinful as long as we have proper attitudes toward them. Let's take a look at some Biblical principles.

★ God will always meet our basic needs of life (Psalm 34:9–10; Matthew 6:31–32; Philippians 4:6 and 19).

★ We should be content with what we have (Philippians 4:11–13; 1 Timothy 6:6; Hebrews 13:5).

★ What we have comes as a gift from God and should be used for His purposes (Matthew 6:19–21, 33; James 1:17).

★ Gaining possessions or positions should not be our primary goal in life (Proverbs 23:4–5; Philippians 3:7–9; 1 Timothy 6:17–19).

★ Pursuing riches and power can destroy our souls (Matthew 6:24; Luke 12:15–21; 1 Timothy 6:7–10; Proverbs 30:8–9).

★ Many things are much more important than possessions and positions (Mark 8:36–37; Proverbs 16:16–17; Proverbs 22:1).

Consider again the words of Mark 8:37. "Or what will a man give in exchange for his soul?" This question could be stated in several ways.

What would you give in exchange for your health?
What would you give in exchange for your family?
What would you give in exchange for a deep sense
of happiness and purpose?
What would you give in exchange for God's blessing
on your life?

Your life has greater importance than the mere collection of possessions. You can serve a greater purpose than filling a position that has no eternal value. Who knows but that you were sent to the kingdom for such a time as this.

INQUIRY-ACTION 19.1

PERSONAL LESSONS FROM THE BOOK OF ESTHER

Write about the three most important lessons you have personally learned from the book of Esther.

1

_____

_____

_____

_____

_____

2

_____

_____

_____

_____

_____

3

_____

_____

_____

_____

INQUIRY-ACTION 19.2

POSSESSIONS AND POSITION
THE LESSONS FOR ME

❖ God will always meet our basic needs of life
(Psalm 34:9–10; Matthew 6:31–32; Philippians 4:6,
19).

❖ We should be content with what we have
(Philippians 4:11–13; 1 Timothy 6:6; Hebrews 13:5).

❖ What we have comes as a gift from God and
should be used for His purposes (Matthew 6:19–21,
33; James 1:17).

❖ Gaining possessions or positions should not be
our primary goal in life (Proverbs 23:4–5; Philippians
3:7–9; 1 Timothy 6:17–19).

Inquiry-Action 19.2 (CONTINUED)

❖   Pursuing riches and power can destroy our souls (Matthew 6:24; Luke 12:15–21; 1 Timothy 6:7–10; Proverbs 30:8–9).

❖   Many things are much more important than possessions and positions (Mark 8:35–37; Proverbs 16:16–17; Proverbs 22:1).

The truths from Mark 8:35-37 that I need to apply to my own life are:

_____

_____

_____

_____

_____

_____

INQUIRY-ACTION 19.3

MARK 8:35–37

Use the Word Bank to help you write the verses.

	gains	lose/loses	
a	give	man	to
after	good	me	wants
and	gospel/gospel's	my	what
but	he	or	will
can	his	own	whoever
desires	if	profit	whole
exchange	in	sake	world
for	is	save	would
forfeit	it	soul	yet
	life	the	

_____

_____

_____

_____

_____

_____

_____

_____

CAIN AND ABEL

Surviving Destructive Anger

Tony and Eric are brothers, and it is not unusual for brothers to become angry with each other. The current squabble began as a simple disagreement over what to watch on television. Before long, unkind words were exchanged, followed by a little pushing and shoving. Anger erupted and a full-blown fight followed. In the scuffle, Eric's shoulder hit the front leg of the table, sending the television crashing to the floor. Not a pretty picture! What was once a simple disagreement became an out-of-control conflict with major consequences.

It is not unusual for brothers (and sisters) to become angry with each other. It all began in the first family. No one really knows all the details behind the story of Cain and Abel. The two may have disagreed often. There could have been some jealousy. Although the facts about their early lives are unknown, the Bible does tell us that Cain eventually became so angry that he killed his brother.

Stop and think about that for a moment. One of the first two brothers recorded in the Bible killed the other brother. Why was Cain so angry? Was it something Abel did or something Cain failed to do? Or was he really mad at God?

The story begins in Genesis 4 where Adam and Eve had two sons. Cain, the older brother, was a farmer. Abel was a shepherd. These were both honorable professions, and when each came to worship God, they brought sacrifices representing their work. However, when Cain offered a sacrifice of what he had produced in the fields, God was not pleased. Instead, God preferred Abel's sacrifice of the firstborn lamb of his flock.

You may be thinking, "How unfair! Each brother brought the best he had. Why was God so displeased with Cain?" The answer lies in Genesis 3. Remember that after Adam and Eve sinned, God killed the first animals in order to make clothing for them. This event shows us that from the very beginning, a covering for sin requires a blood sacrifice. This principle is later found in the laws given to Moses—without blood, there is no forgiveness of sin (Leviticus 17:11). These examples were pictures of Jesus Christ, whose blood takes away the sins of the world (1 John 1:7).

Cain was like many people today who disregard God's requirements and believe that doing their best will satisfy God. He was also like many of us in allowing a bad situation to become worse. Burning in anger, he killed his brother and left his blood lying in the field. Soon the Lord called Cain to account for the first murder in human history: "Where is Abel your brother?" Refusing to accept responsibility for what he had done, Cain claimed no knowledge. "Am I my brother's keeper?" he replied.

Have you ever been caught "in the act" of doing something wrong and then pretending you didn't know anything about it? It was no different with Cain. But God knew the truth. "The voice of your brother's blood cries out to me from the ground," the Lord told him.

Because of his crime, Cain was sentenced to wander the earth. His labors in farming were useless. The ground into which Abel's blood had flowed refused to produce crops for him. Fearing that he would be killed by others, Cain begged for mercy. "My punishment is greater than I can bear," he cried out to God.

God heard his prayer and showed mercy by setting on him a mark that would keep attackers away. The Bible does not explain what this mark was, but many Bible scholars believe it was some sort of skin blemish. The mark was a sign of two things. First, it showed that Cain was a murderer. Second, it was an indication that the Lord himself would repay vengeance sevenfold upon anyone who harmed Cain. For the rest of his life, he had to live with the knowledge that he had killed his brother. His anger had led him to commit the most horrible of crimes.

As you already know, anger is a powerful emotion. There have certainly been a number of times in your life when you have been angry. Did you control your anger? Or did your anger cause you to be destructive toward yourself or others?

Your answer is important. Thousands of criminals are in jails all around the country because they could not control their tempers. Others, who are not behind bars, suffer from broken families and lost opportunities because of their uncontrolled anger. Managing anger in a constructive way is a valuable life skill you can begin learning today.

Ephesians 4:26–27 is probably the most well-known passage in the Bible about anger. "Be angry, and do not sin: do not let the sun go down on your wrath, nor give place to the devil." There are several important principles for us to learn in these verses.

First, anger is a God-given emotion. In itself, it is not sinful. God has given us many emotions—love, fear, guilt, joy, etc. Just as we are to express our other emotions, we are to express our anger. It is almost as if the Bible says, "When you are angry, don't sin." Maybe it's hard for you to believe that it is all right to be angry. Did you know that in the Old Testament "the anger of the Lord" is mentioned at least 18 times? Of course, in the New Testament we learn that Jesus was angry at the moneychangers in the Temple, as well as the religious hypocrites. Anger is justified when God's Word is disobeyed, when sin is present, or people are being hurt. There are times when anger is very appropriate.

The second important principle is that we have the ability to control our responses. We are not helpless victims of our emotions. Return to Genesis 4:7, "If you do well, will you not be accepted? And if you do not do well, sin lies at the door. And its (sin's) desire is for you, but you should rule over it." Cain could have made a choice to rule his anger. Just like us, he was responsible for his response.

Third, our choice of response can show spiritual grace and maturity. Or it can be sinful by either hurting ourselves or hurting others. This is the kind of response that is forbidden in Scripture. "So then, my beloved brethren, let every man be swift to hear, slow to speak, slow to wrath; for the wrath of man does not produce the righteousness of God" (James 1:19–20). Most anger is unjustified. We typically become angry when we don't get our own way or when we jump to conclusions before we have all the facts. This focus on self (the big "I" in SIN) causes us to feel more anger than we should. It also causes us to react in a sinful manner.

Fourth, Ephesians 4:26 cautions us against the two harmful ways of handling anger. These are: don't stow it and don't blow it. The first one is, "Do not let the sun go down on your anger." That's a pretty clear direction. We are not to let our anger carry over to the next day. In New Testament times, the setting of the sun was the closing of the day and the beginning of the next. Before the next day starts, we are to be sure that our anger problem is solved. When we stow our anger internally, our attitudes change. We become resentful, critical and bitter. We cause friends to avoid us. We can even become physically or mentally ill because we have failed to resolve our anger.

The second direction on handling anger is found in the words "do not . . . give place to the devil." The devil's work is always in opposition to God's work. The devil wants to tear down and destroy. When we blow up, we lash out in angry, hurtful words. Or we seek revenge, perhaps ending in physical harm to others. Thus we have promoted the devil's work. Don't let your anger result in the devil getting the best of you. Determine to make the choice to follow God's way in handling your anger.

We can be victorious over anger. Scripture, especially the book of Proverbs, gives several guidelines for us to follow when we become angry.

Guideline 1: Don't be offended by everything that happens.

There are some people who are always looking for a fight. That is not the way a Christian acts. Don't feel like you always have to defend yourself or always be right. Proverbs 19:11 says that "glory" comes to the person who can control his anger when he's been offended. God's love for you (and others) can help you overlook some offenses. Learn to go on with life. Keep a good attitude regardless of what others do.

"The discretion of a man makes him slow to anger, and his glory is to overlook a transgression."

Guideline 2:   Be slow to get angry and be slow to speak.

Take control of your feelings. Don't let them rule you. When you feel yourself becoming angry, count to 10 or 100, breathe deeply, hold your tongue, take a walk, write a letter to yourself, think it through. Ask yourself: What does God want me to learn? How does God want me to respond? What response will best solve the problem?

> *"He who is slow to wrath has great understanding, but he who is impulsive exalts folly." (Proverbs 14:29)*

Guideline 3:   Confess wrong actions of the past and seek wisdom for the future.

God cautions us against trying to confront others' wrongdoing when we have sin in our own lives. Remember that Jesus taught about the speck versus the plank in Matthew 7:3–5. One danger of stowing our anger inside us is that it can erupt later and make our reactions to a small problem greater than they should be. Therefore, we must get rid of all anger, malice and bitterness (Colossians 3:8). God wants us to do the right thing and will provide clear guidance and strength when we determine to go His way.

> *"For the Lord gives wisdom; from His mouth come knowledge and understanding." (Proverbs 2:6)*

Guideline 4:   Don't speak without thinking first.

It has been said that the strongest muscle in the body is not in the leg, but in the tongue. What you say can get you into trouble faster than anything you can do. Therefore, you must be very careful in how you speak. The Bible rules are simple to remember. They are more difficult to obey. Our words must be truthful, loving, gentle, not hasty, carefully chosen and beneficial to others.

> *"A soft answer turns away wrath, but a harsh word stirs up anger."*
> *(Proverbs 15:1)*

"Whoever guards his mouth and tongue, keeps his soul from troubles"
(Proverbs 21:23)

Guideline 5:   Resolve problems quickly.

Have you ever heard someone say, "It's the little things that get on my nerves?" The "little things" have a way over time of becoming major problems. One way of prevention is simple: don't allow the little irritations. When someone does or says something that irritates you, talk to them about it immediately. Don't assume the worst. Be honest about how you feel. If you remove the little irritations on a daily basis, you will take a major step toward avoiding anger.

Full-blown problems need to also be resolved as quickly as possible. Over time, problems can escalate because others become involved, feelings intensify and the positions of those involved become entrenched. What was once a minor disagreement can seem impossible to solve because so many hurtful things have been said and done.

> *"Wrath is cruel and anger a torrent (flood), but who is able to stand*
> *before jealousy? Open rebuke is better than love carefully concealed."*
> *(Proverbs 27:4–5)*

Guideline 6:   Don't be friends with angry people.

If you hang around angry people, their anger will spill over onto you. Anger is contagious! It affects everyone with whom it comes in contact. If you spend time with angry people, heed the words of Proverbs 22:24–25:

> *"Make no friendship with an angry man; and with a furious man do not*
> *go; lest you learn his ways, and set a snare for your soul."*

Anger is an emotion that you will experience throughout your lifetime. It is an emotion that you must learn to control, or it will control you. Anger controlled Cain. Does anger have control of you?

INQUIRY-ACTION 20.1

GROWING THROUGH MY ANGER

1 The top three things that most make me angry are . . .

1) _____

2) _____

3) _____

2 The way I am most likely to handle my own anger is . . .

_____

_____

_____

3 The way I am most likely to respond to those who are angry with me is . . .

_____

_____

_____

4 I have realized that the way I handle anger may be harming me because . . .

_____

_____

_____

INQUIRY–ACTION 20.1 (CONTINUED)

5 I have realized that the way I handle anger may be harming others because . . .

_____

_____

_____

6 Some advice to give myself on managing anger in more constructive ways is . . .

1) _____

2) _____

3) _____

7 A problem related to anger that I plan to work on in the next month is . . .

_____

_____

_____

8 What I hope will happen is . . .

_____

_____

_____

INQUIRY–ACTION 20.2

MANAGING ANGER POSITIVELY

I. Begin with understanding your anger:

A. _____

B. _____

    1. _____

    2. _____

    3. _____

    4. _____

C. _____

    1. _____

    2. _____

    3. _____

* However, you do not have the right to be angry simply because people do not do or say _____.

II. Now, get control of yourself:

A. _____

B. _____

INQUIRY-ACTION 20.2 (CONTINUED)

C. _____

    1. _____

    2. _____

    3. _____

III. Finally, resolve anger positively:

A. _____

B. _____

    1. _____

        a. _____

        b. _____

        c. _____

    2. _____

    3. _____

    4. _____

    5. _____

INQUIRY-ACTION 20.3

EPHESIANS 4:26–27

Use the first letter of each word to help you write the verses.

```
B A A D H S D H
L T S G D O Y
W H G P T T D
```

_____

_____

_____

_____

_____

_____

_____

_____

JONAH

Surviving Wrong Motives

You have heard of the Puritans. They lived during the 16th and 17th centuries in England and New England. They were primarily noted for their simple way of life and strong desire to live purely and godly.

In the early history of America, Salem, Massachusetts, was one of the largest Puritan communities in the world. The residents of the city were known throughout New England for their determination to live holy lives. Accused of a sin, a member would be driven from the community. Sometimes the punishment was far worse. However, if the member confessed his sin, he could be forgiven and received back into the community.

The real problem in Salem was this: What did you do if you were accused of a sin that you really did not commit? Did you lie and say you were guilty in order to remain in the community? Or did you tell the truth—proclaim your innocence—and be banned from the community or executed? Obviously, great power lay in the hands of the accusers. This is apparent in the historical event known as the Salem Witch Trials.

In the winter of 1692, a number of parents were concerned about the spiritual condition of their children. As a result, the minister began a series of religious revival meetings. At the same time, a few of the young girls began to meet secretly with the minister's slave, Tituba. As a Carib Indian, Tituba had grown up believing in magic and spirit worship. She told the young Puritan girls stories about her ancestors, magic and witchcraft. Soon the girls began to exhibit a number of strange behaviors. The pastor did all he could to calm them, but the problem only grew worse.

What happened next was one of the saddest events in America's history. The girls began to accuse several women in the community of witchcraft. NO ONE KNOWS WHY!

It was not long before over a hundred innocent people came under suspicion. The accused had only two options. They could confess in a court trial to a sin that they had not committed and be thus restored to the community. Or, they could truthfully deny the accusation and be banned or executed by the civil authorities. The hysteria increased, and between June 10 and September 22, nineteen men and women were hanged for witchcraft. One of the accused, Giles Corey, was pressed to death between rocks. When given one last chance to save himself, he simply said, "More weight."

Twenty years later the girls confessed to the false accusations that they had made. But it was too late. Twenty people had been executed, others died in prison and countless families had been destroyed. Many have speculated as to why these girls accused the men and women of witchcraft. But there are no answers; their motives are still unknown.

A motive is a "feeling or desire that causes us to act." Sometimes a motive is very natural, almost mechanical. For example, if you are very thirsty and in need of water, you are highly motivated to find something to drink. If you are suddenly confronted by danger, you are motivated to protect yourself and find safety. In both cases, your motive is to survive. You don't have to think very long about what you need to do.

However, most of what we do is not an automatic response to a situation. There are many things we deliberately do or say. Our words and deeds are not driven by natural responses, but by conscious decisions. Have you ever spoken to someone in an unkind way? Certainly, you have. The words you used were not an accident. They were the result of a conscious decision. Once you have answered the question "Why did I say those unkind things?," you have determined the motive for your actions.

Most people don't stop and think about their personal motives. This certainly had to be true for the prophet Jonah. The book of Jonah is not just a story about a great fish who swallowed a disobedient prophet. It is also the account of a man who made ungodly decisions because he was influenced by wrong motives.

The tale begins with the Lord's command to Jonah: "Arise, go to Nineveh, that great city, and cry against it; for their wickedness has come up before me." But Jonah disobeyed God and boarded a ship for Tarshish. By going to Tarshish, Jonah hoped to travel as far away from Nineveh as possible.

Of course, Jonah was swallowed by the great fish. But why was Jonah disobedient in the first place? What was his motive for refusing to obey God and then running from Him? The answers to those questions are found in Jonah 4:1–3.

After God released Jonah from the great fish, Jonah went to Nineveh as God had originally told him to do. He warned the leaders and inhabitants of Ninevah that God would destroy them if they did not repent of their evil ways. According to 3:5–10, the people did repent of their sins and God spared the city.

Jonah's worst nightmare had come true! God was not going to punish the nation that had so frequently attacked and humiliated Israel. Jonah was very angry. Then, in 4:2, he revealed his motive for fleeing to Tarshish the first time God commanded him to go to Nineveh.

> "... Ah Lord, was not this what I said when I was still in my
> country? Therefore I fled previously to Tarshish; for I know that
> You are a gracious and merciful God, slow to anger and abundant
> in lovingkindness, One who relents from doing harm."

Simply stated, Jonah said, "God, I knew You would do it! I knew that if I went to Nineveh, they would repent of their sins and You would spare them. Because you are gracious, merciful, slow to anger and full of kindness, I knew you would forgive them. Then you would not destroy them, and my prophecies would seem foolish."

That was Jonah's motive for running from God. He wanted revenge on Nineveh. He wanted God to punish them for their wickedness. The last thing in the world he wanted was for them to be spared. So, he ran away from God.

Wrong motives will always get us into trouble and lead us down a pathway of sin. Our motives are the result of what is important to us. Whatever is important to us will motivate us to action. This important principle can be shown in the following way:

$$I \rightarrow M \rightarrow A$$

The "I" stands for what is IMPORTANT to us. The "M" represents our MOTIVES. The "A" stands for our ACTIONS.

This principle is clearly taught in Proverbs 23:7: "For as he (a man) thinks in his heart, so is he . . ." God's Word tells us that our actions and words reflect what we think about. And what do we think about? The things that are important to us! So, what's important to you? A new CD or better grades? Pleasing your parents or fitting in with your friends? Doing what you want or doing what God wants?

Right actions based on right motives based on right thinking—this is God's way. That is why it is so important to follow the advice of Philippians 4:8.

> *"Finally, brethren, whatever things are true, whatever things are noble, whatever things are just, whatever things are pure, whatever things lovely, whatever things are of good report, if there is any virtue and if there is anything praiseworthy—meditate on these things."*

If you want to avoid wrong motives, the Apostle Paul tells you to "think on these things." What you think about is what is important to you. What is important to you is what will motivate you. What motivates you will guide your words and actions.

What are you thinking about today?

INQUIRY-ACTION 21.1

JONAH

Read the complete book, then summarize the events following each phrase.

1:2 Arise, go

1:3 But Jonah

1:4 But the Lord

1:5 Then the mariners

1:5 But Jonah

1:6 So the captain

1:9 Then he (Jonah) said

1:15 So they picked up Jonah

INQUIRY-ACTION 21.1 (CONTINUED)

1:17 Now the Lord

_____

2:1 Then Jonah prayed

_____

3:1 Now the word of the Lord came

_____

3:3 So Jonah arose

_____

3:5 So the people of Nineveh

_____

3:10 Then God saw

_____

4:1 But Jonah

_____

4:6 And the Lord God

_____

_____

_____

INQUIRY-ACTION 21.2

Dear Self,

It was good to study the story of Jonah. I learned about the dangers of _____

_____

_____

_____

I think Jonah's experiences can help me in the following ways:

1) _____

_____

2) _____

_____

3) _____

_____

Sincerely,

Self

INQUIRY-ACTION 21.3

"I" STANDS FOR IMPORTANT

List three things that are important to you and what actions they
motivate. Then list God's desires related to each area.

It's important to me . . .	Therefore I often . . .	What God thinks is important is . . .
1		
2		
3		

INQUIRY-ACTION 21.4

PROVERBS 16:2–3

Fill in the words of the verses in the crossword puzzle form without repeating any words. Then write the verses below.

PAUL

Surviving Life Changes

• IN A MATTER OF MOMENTS the fire leaped from the rooftop of the house next door to Susan's home. She had watched the fire move quickly down the canyon all morning. Nothing seemed to stand in its way. Her family hosed down the roof and the sides of their house in hopes that the fire would be deflected. But their roof was now fully engulfed in flames. The end had come.

Susan thought about the many things in her room that she would never see again. She wondered where they would live until they could rebuild their home. She thought about her friends down the street, knowing that their houses had burned to the ground nearly two hours earlier. As she watched her home turn to ashes, she thought about the many changes that were about to take place in her life.

• IN A MATTER OF MOMENTS the doors to the moving van would be closed and locked tight. Ann and her family would then begin the long drive from Tulsa to Boston. Her father's promotion had sounded so exciting. That is, until she realized that it meant relocating in Boston. It all seemed like a dream. Ann was born in Tulsa. She was ready to start high school next year. Now she would have to leave it all—her friends, familiar places and fond memories.

Boston would be radically different from Tulsa. The city was much larger, the weather was much colder; and the way people talked, well, that's another story. New friends, new school and a new church were just a few of the changes that had been forced upon her.

• IN A MATTER OF MOMENTS the uneventful drive to the neighborhood store had turned to tragedy. John had gone with his mother to pick up a few things before dinner. The grocery store was only three miles away. They didn't even have to get on the freeway. As the red light changed to green, their car moved forward through the intersection. And then, out of nowhere, the 18-wheeler appeared. There was no way the crash could be avoided. Before there was even time to think, the truck plowed into the side of their car.

From that point on, John didn't remember a thing. The next face he saw was his father's. The IV tubes and monitors told him that he was in the hospital. Although he couldn't make out everything his father was saying, he understood that he and his mom would be all right. But how long would it take? What would the recovery process be like? Was there a chance that he had suffered some type of permanent damage? He knew that his life had now been changed forever.

• IN A MATTER OF MOMENTS . . . everything changed for Susan, Ann and John. Sometimes change happens like that. Events in your life take such a dramatic turn that you hardly know what hit you. Other times, events are more slowly paced. Either way, responding to life changes can create enormous stress. We are forced from our comfort and security and thrust into unknown territory. Going back is not an option—we have to face the future. Our choice is to become bitter, or better, because of the challenges we face.

The Apostle Paul survived (and thrived) through several dramatic life changes. Formerly known as Saul, he was a Greek-speaking Jew. Not only was he brought up in the strict observance of the Hebrew faith, but he was also a Pharisee, born a Roman citizen, earned his living as a tentmaker and was one of the most well educated men of his time.

But in a matter of moments, the entire course of his life changed. Paul, on his way to Damascus to threaten and imprison Christians, saw a great light from Heaven. As he fell to the ground, he heard a voice calling him by name, "Saul, Saul, why are you persecuting Me?" (Acts 9:4).

As a result of his encounter with the Lord, Paul was blinded for three days. With the help of his traveling companions, he continued on to Damascus. There he was to meet Ananias and receive further instructions. Paul did as he was told. No longer would he persecute God's people.

In response to Paul's question, "Lord, what do You want me to do?", the Lord responded, "You shall be a chosen vessel of Mine to bear My name before Gentiles, kings, and the children of Israel. Therefore, I have appeared to you for this purpose, to make you a minister and a witness both of the things which you have seen and of the things which I will yet reveal to you . . . the Gentiles, to whom I now send you, to open their eyes and to turn them from darkness to light, from the power of Satan to God, that they may receive forgiveness of sins and an inheritance among those who are sanctified by faith in Me" (Acts 9:15; 26:16–18).

Although this dramatic event redirected his life, Paul still faced many other changes throughout his ministry. Shortly after his conversion, Paul preached his first sermon. Soon he met his new coworkers. Later God called him to preach to the Gentiles. Over the next few years, he made three missionary journeys to the newly-established churches throughout the region. At the close of his life, he was imprisoned in a Roman jail.

Paul summarized his experiences in 2 Corinthians 4:6–10, 16–18. "For it is the God who commanded light to shine out of darkness who has shone in our hearts to give the light of the knowledge of the glory of God in the face Jesus Christ. But we have this treasure in earthen vessels, that the excellence of the power may be of God and not of us.

"We are hard pressed on every side, yet not crushed; we are perplexed, but not in despair; persecuted, but not forsaken; struck down, but not destroyed—always carrying about in the body the dying of the Lord Jesus, that the life of Jesus also may be manifested in our body. Therefore, we do not lose heart. Even though our outward man (body) is perishing, yet the inward man (spirit) is being renewed day by day.

"For our light affliction, which is but for a moment, is working for us a far more exceeding and eternal weight of glory, while we do not look at things which are seen, but at the things which are not seen. For the things which are seen are temporary, but the things which are not seen are eternal."

Most people never experience the kinds of changes that Paul faced during his lifetime. However, all people encounter times of change throughout the course of their lives. There will be dramatic times of change like Paul's conversion on the road to Damascus. And there will be less dramatic experiences like meeting new people, changing jobs or moving.

Whether great or small, change is always unsettling. However, the changes we face in our lives should not be feared or avoided. Change is an opportunity for personal growth. We can only grow wiser and more confident as we learn to accept the changes demanded of us. Many of the biographies of great people prove this point. Those who learned how to adapt to change early in life became changers of the world in their later lives.

Think for a moment about some of the changes you and your friends have faced or may face very soon. One of the most common, and most difficult, changes occurs when your family has to move—adjusting to a new environment, going to a new school and making new friends. Other changes occur as the result of a family tragedy. Severe illness, death or divorce are just a few of the tragedies that affect every member of a family. There are also the personal changes that occur as you mature. In making the transition from a child to an adult, the changes can seem overwhelming. In addition to the physical changes you face, you are required to make more decisions, expected to be more responsible, and are faced with determining your future.

Although it is normal to fear or try to avoid the changes we face, the Bible teaches us four important principles about these changes.

Principle 1: God is never surprised by change. This principle should be obvious. Since one of God's characteristics is omniscience (knowing all things), it is impossible for Him to not know about a change that is going to take place in your life. Sometimes you can expect a certain change. On other occasions you can be completely surprised when a change occurs. However, in both cases, God has full knowledge of what is happening. He will never be taken by surprise. In fact, God is in complete control of every change. In addition to being omniscient, God is also omnipotent (possessing all power). The changes you face in your life are under His control. As Christians, we can be confident that there will be some benefit for us in these changes.

Principle 2: The Christian's life is especially based on change. From the moment we turn to Christ, we begin a life-long process of developing the characteristics of Christ in our lives. This involves a day-to-day conformance to the character of Christ. In other words, we choose God's way over our own. Finally, in the resurrection, we will be fully changed to become citizens of Heaven.

Principle 3: God has a purpose for the changes we face. Abraham, Moses, Job, Jonah, Peter, Paul and so many others learned valuable lessons from the changes they experienced during their lives. Think of your life as a journey. Throughout your journey you will experience many happy times, as well as face many difficult challenges. As you encounter and survive each challenge you face, you will learn a lesson you could not have learned without going through the experience.

Principle 4: We should have a right attitude toward change. Wishing for the past only prolongs our negative feelings. We need to work through our emotions, then be flexible and positive about the new opportunities before us.

Welcome the next change that comes into your life. It is an opportunity to mature personally and spiritually. Change is God's way of reminding you that He is working in your life.

INQUIRY-ACTION 22.1

GOD'S LIFE PLAN FOR ME

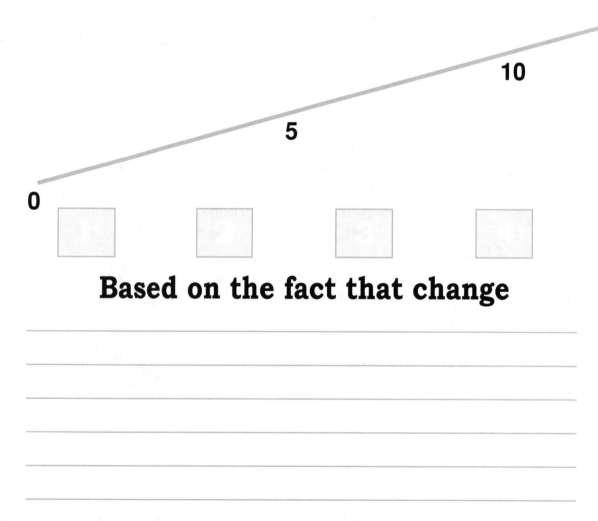

0   5   10

Based on the fact that change

_____

_____

_____

_____

_____

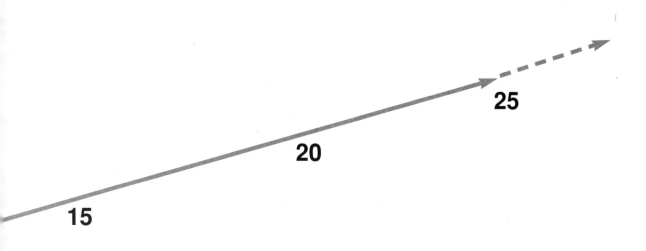

15   20   25

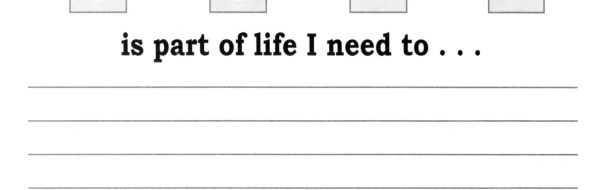

5   6   7   8

is part of life I need to . . .

_____

_____

_____

_____

_____

_____

INQUIRY-ACTION 22.2

PHILIPPIANS 4:12–13

Cross off all extra letters and write the verses.

ike no why owl at obeab asked andiok in
owho what oabo understood eve cryed when
are andi and pall the kings in owhoa ever late
are ned or abbot hot on beef dull can ditto
abes chung dry before that oab goes under
band's toes muffs ernee dipped candy on
pall the kings they brought chris straw hof
string then got her nosey men

_____

_____

_____

_____

_____

_____

JACOB

Surviving Habits of Deception

It was Kevin's first trip to Africa. He could not contain his excitement as he departed for the airport. Soon he would join other teens in an effort to install a water well in a village south of Nairobi. This would be the "trip of a lifetime." Although Kevin had traveled out of the country before, traveling to Africa was a big adventure. He was glad to be going with Stephen Moss. As an experienced world traveler and missions director, he had been to Africa many times. Kevin didn't have to worry about laws, customs or language; Mr. Moss would know exactly what to do.

By the time they reached Nairobi, they had traveled for more than 21 hours. The arrival at the airport was uneventful. However, their trip to the hotel was an entirely different story. Kevin had never experienced the sights, sounds and SMELLS! of a country like Kenya. Although the people were very friendly, they were also in great need—not only of food and simple possessions, but also in spiritual need.

Kevin learned a lot over the two weeks that he and the other teens slept on hard dirt floors, ate native food and worked from dawn to dusk digging the well. However, it was on the third day of his trip that he learned his greatest lesson.

Kevin and Mr. Moss were walking to the customs office to try to secure the release of the pumping equipment that had been shipped months ago. Kevin noticed a band of beggars happily conversing until they saw the two foreigners. Suddenly all conversation ceased, and a hand extended toward Kevin silently pleading for alms. The other hand pulled up a pants' leg to expose a gross, oozing ulcer that would eventually eat away the flesh until it reached the bone. There would then be no hope of cure; the beggar would lose his leg.

Kevin's first reaction was pity. The leg needed to be washed and medicine applied. Surely, someone must help this man! At this point Mr. Moss took Kevin's hand and quickly moved him across the street. As they continued to their destination, Mr. Moss explained that the beggar did not want to be healed. He made his living from his wound. The missionary doctors were willing treat him, and medicines were available at the clinic. Rather than seek treatment, the beggar chose to deceive foreign visitors into thinking that he had no hope.

As a result of his affliction the beggar sought pity, which resulted in more money from those who passed him on the street. Although poor and uneducated, the beggar knew how to practice deceit. He was living a lie.

The two weeks quickly came to an end, and the teens celebrated with the villagers when the new well successfully pumped its first stream of clear, cool water. At home, Kevin only had to turn a faucet, but here the village well would save the natives a five-hour walk each day as they hauled water to and from the river. Kevin was glad he had been a part of the project and could hardly wait to share his experiences with his family and friends.

His encounter with the beggar became his most repeated story. It was hard to believe that someone would refuse treatment. It was even harder to believe that someone would use his ailment as a means of gaining sympathy, and subsequently more money. Kevin was not accustomed to such blatant deceit.

Although you probably don't know anyone who uses an open wound to secure pity and money, you do know people who practice deceit. In fact, deceitful words and actions may be a pattern in your own life right now. Being deceitful is a serious matter. According to Proverbs 6:16–19, lying is one of the seven things God hates. God is the Truth-Teller. Therefore, all deceit is in opposition to His nature. Those who practice deceit belong to their father, the devil, Jesus said.

Solomon once wrote: "He who walks in integrity walks securely, but he who perverts his ways will become known" (Proverbs 10:9). Let's take a close look at that verse. Focus your attention on the word "integrity." A person who walks with integrity walks consistently with the truth. Integrity is the opposite of deceit. A person who is deceitful causes others to accept as true that which is false.

Now focus your attention on the word "securely." To be secure is to be safe. Truth never changes. It produces a strong foundation on which to build confidence. When others know that you will always tell the truth, they don't doubt or question what you say. Because they can trust you, you have greater freedom to do things on your own. That's the reason Jesus said, "You will know the truth and the truth will set you free" (John 8:32).

In the last part of Proverbs 10:9, Solomon tells us that those who walk securely don't worry about being "found out." Solomon knew that if you don't tell the truth, then you have to continue to tell lies to cover up the lies you have already told. Eventually, your lies will be found out and you will have to suffer the consequences of your sins. Your loss of integrity results in loss of security (trust) which results in the loss of privileges (freedoms).

Strong relationships with others require:

Truth ➡ **Trust** ➡ **Freedom**

Broken relationships result from:

Deceit ➡ **Distrust** ➡ **Discipline or loss of friendship**

Every day you make choices about how you will live, whether with integrity or deceit. Based on your choices, you can earn respect from others, or earn their dislike. Galatians 6:7 puts it this way: "Do not be deceived, God is not mocked; for whatever a man sows, that he will also reap." In other words, if you are deceitful you will eventually pay a great price for your deception.

That's what happened in Jacob's life. You remember him as one of the patriarchs of the Old Testament. These were men who headed the nation of Israel and received the promises of God to become the family of Christ. However, they were not perfect people. You have already studied some of the struggles faced by Abraham and Isaac. Jacob and Esau were the twin sons of Isaac. Later Jacob became the father of the twelve sons (including Joseph) who headed the tribes of Israel.

Jacob's name means supplanter or deceiver. Even before birth he and Esau struggled against each other. Never have two boys been more different. Esau was first-born and the pride of his aging father. With a ruddy, strong appearance he became a skilled hunter. Jacob was the favorite of his mother Rebekah. One day Jacob had cooked a large pot of stew and some fresh bread. Esau came home from the fields near starvation and agreed to sell his "birthright" in exchange for stew. Thus, the enmity continued to grow between the brothers.

God had revealed to Rebekah that Jacob, the younger of the twins, was to become the next leader of the family. However, she was unwilling to wait for God's plan. Instead, she initiated her own plan of deceit the day she overheard Isaac talking about giving the "Blessing" to Esau. Related to the birthright, the "Blessing" established the right of inheritance and family leadership. Because her husband was nearly blind, he would be unable to tell the difference between the two sons. She could fool him into thinking that Jacob was actually Esau. With Jacob's help, she put the plan into motion. Isaac was deceived and Jacob received the "Blessing."

As a result of the deception, Jacob fled to the city of Haran to live with his uncle Laban. You have studied the story of Rachel and Leah. Remember that after Jacob worked seven years to gain his beautiful young cousin Rachel, Laban switched brides and Jacob married Leah. He had to work another seven years for the right to marry Rachel. Laban again deceived Jacob in dividing the flocks. Jacob, the deceiver, learned some hard lessons about being the object of deception.

Finally, Jacob made the most important decision of his life—to return home and make things right with Esau. On the way Jacob spent the night near the brook of

Jabbok. Throughout the night he wrestled with a Man sent from God. When morning's light broke, Jacob refused to release the Man until he had received God's blessing. In that instant Jacob's heart change was reflected in his name change. The Man of God renamed him Israel, Prince with God. Jacob left the brook with a permanent limp, a constant reminder that he was no longer a self-sufficient, conniving deceiver, but a reflection of God's nature. Jacob—renamed Israel—became a man of integrity and security.

That brings us back to our story about the beggar. Although medical care and medicines were available, he did not want to be healed. He chose a life of deception instead of a life of truth-telling.

Is that your choice? Do you regularly deceive others? Are you caught in such a complex web of deception that you don't even know how to escape? It is time to break loose from a life of lies and deception.

The decision is up to you.

INQUIRY–ACTION 23.1

JACOB, THE DECEIVER

Read and summarize each topic listed based on the references provided.

I. Jacob's Family
  A. His parents (Genesis 25:19–20)

  B. The promise to Isaac (Genesis 26:2–4)

  C. The prophecy about Jacob (Genesis 25:22–23)

  D. The twins (Genesis 25:24–26)

II. Jacob Gains the Birthright from Esau
  A. Characteristics of the twins (Genesis 25:27–28)

  B. Deception of Esau (Genesis 25:29–34)

III. Isaac Gives His Blessing
  A. Isaac's plan (Genesis 27:1–7)

  B. Rebekah's plan (Genesis 27:8–17)

  C. Jacob's deceit (Genesis 27:18–30)

  D. Esau's response (Genesis 27:31–41)

  E. Jacob's escape (Genesis 27:42–45; 28:10–22)

INQUIRY-ACTION 23.2

JACOB, THE DECEIVER (CONTINUED)

Read and summarize each topic listed based on the references provided.

IV. Jacob Meets His Match
  A. The agreement (Genesis 29:1–4, 9–10, 12–15, 18–21)

  B. The betrayal (Genesis 29:23–25)

  C. The second agreement (Genesis 29:26–28)

  D. The third agreement (Genesis 30:27–28, 32, 36)

  E. Jacob's continuing deception (Genesis 30:42–43; 31:1–2)

  F. Laban's continuing deception (Genesis 31:4–7)

V. Jacob Heads Home
  A. Jacob sneaks away (Genesis 31:17–20)

  B. Rachel deceives her father (Genesis 31:25–26, 30–32, 34–35, 41–42, 55)

  C. Jacob sends gifts (Genesis 32:13–18)

VI. Jacob Meets the Lord
  A. Jacob wrestles an angel (Genesis 32:24–26, 32)

  B. Jacob becomes Israel (Genesis 32:27–29)

  C. Jacob receives forgiveness (Genesis 33:4–12)

INQUIRY–ACTION 23.3

PROVERBS' PRESCRIPTIONS FOR BECOMING A TRUTH-TELLER

I. **Talk Less.** *(Proverbs 10:8, 10, 19; 13:3; 17:27; 21:23; 29:30; see Ecclesiastes 5:2 and 6:11)*

II. **Tell the Truth Even if It Costs You.** *(Proverbs 4:24; 12:9; 21:3; 27:5–6; 28:6, 23)*

III. **The Moment You Realize You Have Been Less than Truthful, Return to the Person and Make It Right.** *(Proverbs 12:18–20; 16:13; 20:3, 7; 21:3, 21; 28:13)*

IV. **Be Alert to Subsequent Temptations to Deceive Others, and Resist Them.** *(Proverbs 1:23; 2:3–6, 10–11; 3:5–6; 8:6–7; 13:3; 21:23; see also Psalms 39:1 and 141:3–4)*

INQUIRY-ACTION 23.4

PSALM 34:12–14 (1 PETER 3:10–11)

Locate all the words in the Word Find and write the verses below

```
D E E H D N A M Y A M S L O V E T H A T
M F Y T N S G O O D S P I L F R O M N H
A R O E A E N R U T S E V I L A P R R K
Y O U R T I I F R E E S E F P E U L E D
O M R I E L K Y R G U I L E E T R E V E
H R O S A O A H W E X M I K A H S N E C
W U F E N V E T A H T A U T C E U G O E
G O O D D E P A R T O N G U E R E T H I
M Y A N D S S Y A D S Y M K I T A H W T
Y N A M S E R I S E D N A N D O F R O M
```

_____

_____

_____

_____

_____

_____

_____

_____

_____

DEBORAH

Surviving Unrealistic Expectations

Have you ever watched the seventh game of a World Series? What makes the game so exciting is that the series is tied, three games apiece. Everything is now on the line. When this game is over, the World Championship will have been decided.

Now, fast-forward nine innings. The game is over. It was a close contest, but the World Champion has now been announced. Like everyone else, you look forward to hearing what the manager has to say about this exciting win. Finally, he appears on screen. After thanking his players, he makes the following bold announcement:

"We are the greatest baseball team that has ever played the game. There is no finer group of ballplayers in the world. So, I am announcing today that our team will win the World Series for the next ten years in a row."

What would be your response to such a statement? "Did he really say that? Is he joking? Is he crazy?" His comments would shock you and everyone else. No one in his right mind would make such a claim. It would be such an unrealistic expectation that no one would believe it.

Although not quite to this extreme, there are people who have unrealistic expectations of you. Sometimes the unrealistic expectations come from friends or family. All too often, individuals hold unrealistic expectations for themselves. The following story clearly illustrates what an unrealistic expectation is.

One day a father and his daughter were taking a ride through the country. Although the roads were worn and narrow, it was great to be away from the thousands of cars that were on the freeway. Both the father and daughter were enjoying the refreshing and peaceful drive. All of a sudden, the little girl saw a large object on top of a fence post.

"Pull over, Daddy, pull over," she said. "I want to see what that is." As her father brought the car slowly to a stop, the little girl hopped out and ran toward the fence post. "What is it?" she asked. All she could see was this odd-shaped object that looked a little like a rock with moving legs.

"It's a turtle, honey," her father said. "Someone placed a turtle on top of this fence post."

"How do you know that someone put him there?" she challenged. "He has legs, he could have climbed the fence post all by himself." Her dad laughed at his daughter's limited experience as he gently placed the turtle back on the ground and headed him toward a nearby stream.

The little girl certainly had unrealistic expectations for that turtle. If you have ever closely observed a turtle, and are familiar with the height of a fence post, you will agree that turtles can't climb fence posts! It would be unrealistic to believe that any turtle could (or would want to) accomplish that feat.

Do you ever feel that you are expected to do the impossible? Do you sometimes wonder if you have the ability to achieve even your own hopes and dreams? Maybe you feel like a turtle sitting on a fence post. Everyone expects that you can get down on your own, but you don't see how. You just don't know how to survive these unrealistic expectations.

Deborah, an Old Testament prophetess and judge, faced a similar problem. She had to overcome the unrealistic expectations that the people of Israel had of her. Before you can understand how she did it, you need to know a little more about her life and what had happened to her people.

Deborah was the fourth judge whose stories are told in the book of Judges. These "judges" not only provided counsel in order to settle disputes, they were expected to serve as military leaders. It is important to remember that Deborah was the only woman judge in a group of 13 judges who ruled Israel for 430 years.

The nation of Israel suffered under the oppression of the Canaanites, led by King Jabin. Day after day, Deborah learned of the difficult conditions experienced by her people. Not only did they seek her judgment, they also looked to her to deliver them from the Canaanites. But were the people of Israel expecting too much of her? How would she accomplish this seemingly impossible task? Was it right for the nation to expect her to stand up against the mighty Canaanites who had an army of 900 chariots and many thousands of soldiers?

Was Israel's expectation unrealistic? Consider the following challenges she faced and then you be the judge.

Challenge 1: She was a long way from the Canaanites. Deborah was a judge in the southern part of Israel, the Canaanites were located in the north. If she was going to defeat the enemy, she and her army would have to travel a considerable distance.

Challenge 2: She was not a trained warrior. How would she be able to train troops when she knew nothing about fighting? Even if they were trained, how would weapons and other resources be obtained?

Challenge 3: It was not a woman's place to lead an army. Even if she under-stood warfare and knew how to assemble an army, she would not be able to serve as its leader. She would have to find a man who was willing and capable of providing the necessary military leadership.

Challenge 4: The Canaanites had a superior army. The people of Israel were farmers and shepherds. How could they be trained to wage war against professional soldiers? Even with months of training, Israel would not stand a chance.

Challenge 5: Deborah was faced with the nation's fear and lack of faith in God.
Would Barak, who was also afraid, be able to overcome his fears and lead this nation to military victory? Would men be willing to risk their lives in the face of overwhelming obstacles?

Was Israel's expectation of Deborah unrealistic? After considering the challenges facing her, it would surely seem like it. But she did live up to their expectations. She and Barak formed an army of Israelites that defeated the Canaanites. As a result, the people of Israel were delivered from their enemy and enjoyed 40 years of peace.

How was Deborah able to be victorious, in spite of such overwhelming odds? The answer is found in the chapter following the story of Israel's victory over the Canaanites. In Judges 5, Deborah sang a song of praise to God for His goodness to the nation.

> *"When the leaders lead in Israel, when the people willingly offer themselves, bless the Lord!"* (Judges 5:2)

The victory began when Deborah willingly offered herself to do God's will. Even though it seemed that victory over the Canaanites was an impossible task, she was willing to obey God. Because of her willingness to offer herself, Barak agreed to lead the troops. Although he was afraid, Deborah convinced him to trust God. When the nation saw that Deborah and Barak willingly offered themselves, they also responded in obedience.

As you read Judges 4, you learn that it was not the mighty army of Israel or the great leadership of Deborah and Barak that ultimately defeated the Canaanites. It was God Who, in a very unusual way, made it possible for Israel's army to be victorious.

However, it all began with one person by the name of Deborah. She survived unrealistic expectations and overwhelming odds because she was willing to offer herself to God in complete obedience.

Maybe it's not all that bad to be a turtle on a fence post. One thing is for sure, when you're sitting on top of a post, you know that you are not the one in control! Survival is possible only when someone bigger than you steps into the picture. What an opportunity to see God working in your life!

That's what we need to remember when we face the expectations of others. All the Lord asks is that we willingly offer ourselves to Him. When we let Him take control of our lives, we will be victorious over the challenges we face—even climbing down from a fence post.

Inquiry-Action 24.1

Do-Nothing Bingo

Ask a classmate to sign or initial any block that accurately describes his or her actions in the last two weeks. An individual's initials can only go on your paper one time.

☐	I have not been to youth Bible study.
☐	I have not exercised outside of a sport or P. E. class.
☐	I have not had a long heart-to-heart conversation with my parents.
☐	I have not read a non-fiction book that was not assigned at school or church.
☐	I have not volunteered to help people in my church or community.
☐	I have not been out of bed before 6:00 A.M. more than twice.
☐	I have not tried a totally new hobby or activity.
☐	I have not written a letter to a person who really likes hearing from me.
☐	I have not purposely saved more than $2.00.
☐	I have not watched less than an hour of television each day, on average.
☐	I have not offered to help my parents with house cleaning beyond my normal chores.
☐	I have not volunteered to care for younger brothers or sisters at home or children belonging to family friends, my teachers or at church.
☐	I have not worked with my friends to clean up or improve the neighborhood.
☐	I have not helped my pastor with calls, visitation or preparation for Bible study.
☐	I have not worked to earn my own spending money.
☐	I have not volunteered to help a teacher or other school official for more than a task that requires less than five minutes.

INQUIRY-ACTION 24.2

GREAT EXPECTATIONS

Write a list of the expectations you believe the people named have of you.
Circle "R" for all that seem *reasonable*. Circle "D" for those that are *difficult*
but do-able. Circle "U" for those that seem totally *unrealistic*.

Teachers	Parents
1. _____ R D U	1. _____ R D U
2. _____ R D U	2. _____ R D U
3. _____ R D U	3. _____ R D U
4. _____ R D U	4. _____ R D U
5. _____ R D U	5. _____ R D U
6. _____ R D U	6. _____ R D U
7. _____ R D U	7. _____ R D U
8. _____ R D U	8. _____ R D U

INQUIRY-ACTION 24.2 (CONTINUED)

GREAT EXPECTATIONS

Write a list of the expectations you believe the people named have of you.
Circle "R" for all that seem *reasonable*. Circle "D" for those that are *difficult*
but do-able. Circle "U" for those that seem totally *unrealistic*.

Friends	Myself
1. _____ R D U	1. _____ R D U
2. _____ R D U	2. _____ R D U
3. _____ R D U	3. _____ R D U
4. _____ R D U	4. _____ R D U
5. _____ R D U	5. _____ R D U
6. _____ R D U	6. _____ R D U
7. _____ R D U	7. _____ R D U
8. _____ R D U	8. _____ R D U

INQUIRY-ACTION 24.3

MANAGING UNREALISTIC EXPECTATIONS
PRINCIPLES FROM THE LIFE OF DEBORAH

1

2

3

4

5

INQUIRY-ACTION 24.4

MATTHEW 11:28–30

motion forefinger toward self

point to self

point to others

mime working

mime carrying large object   ,

point to self

point to others

mime napping   .

grab air with fist

point to self

mime barbells across shoulders

point to others

mime reading a book

point to self   ,

question look on face

point to self

pet a pretend animal

drop shoulders, hold head down

pat upper left chest   ,

point to others

mime locating lost object

mime napping

fold hands over heart   .

question look on face

point to self

mime barbells across shoulders

mime throwing light object

mime carrying large object

mime pitching cotton ball in air   .

MOSES

Surviving Personal Inadequacies

The frantic call came about 1:33 p.m. When Dan Peterson picked up the telephone, he recognized the voice of his neighbor at the other end. He knew immediately that there was something terribly wrong.

"Dan," the neighbor said, "you must come home, NOW!"

"What's the matter?" Mr. Peterson anxiously asked as he rose from his chair to make his way to the office door.

"Your house is on fire and little Jimmy is trapped in his upstairs bedroom. We can't get him out!"

As Mr. Peterson made his way to his car to drive the four-mile trip home, he was completely unaware of how hard his neighbors and the local fire department were working to save his son. The fire had engulfed the inside of the house, preventing any hope of escape down the stairs. The only chance for Jimmy's survival was out the bedroom window, to a waiting net nearly 20 feet below. However, Jimmy could not see the net. The thick, billowing smoke made it impossible to see what was down below.

Even through the smoke and flames, Jimmy knew that a crowd had gathered below. Along with the firemen, everyone was yelling, "Jump! Jump!" Frozen with fear, the young boy was not able to make the jump that could save his life.

Over a loudspeaker he heard the voice of what he assumed to be a fireman. "The only way you'll survive is if you jump. We've spread out a safety net. You'll be perfectly safe. You must jump. You must jump now!"

As the crowd continued to yell, Jimmy still didn't have the courage to make the jump. His feet were cemented to the floor. Then, over the loudspeaker came a familiar voice. It was his dad.

"It's okay son, you can do it. You can jump," came the calm voice of his father. As the words of his father reached him, Jimmy's fear dissolved. The trust and love that had been established between them gave him the courage to do what he had to do—jump blindly into the dark smoke to the waiting safety net below.

This story, in modern context, illustrates an old and familiar story found in the book of Exodus—the life of Moses. Moses is probably one of the best known characters in the Bible.

When the name of Moses is mentioned, which incident in his life comes to your mind? Did you think about the ten plagues and his confrontation with Pharaoh? Do you wonder what it was like the day he led the entire nation of Israel out of Egypt and Pharaoh's army drowned in the Red Sea? Perhaps your mind immediately pictures the meeting of Moses with God on Mount Sinai.

In addition to these "big" events, there were the provision of manna, the bronze serpent, and Moses' faithfulness to lead the nation through the wilderness to the Promised Land. When you think of Moses, you probably think of a confident leader who was unafraid to challenge even the great Pharaoh of Egypt.

But that's not the way it was at the beginning. Think about the Burning Bush incident in Exodus 3 and 4. When Moses was first given the assignment by God to go to Pharaoh and demand Israel's release, he openly questioned the wisdom of God's decision.

Moses reminded God that he was too inadequate to ever accomplish what God had asked him to do. First of all, his **past** was inadequate. You remember the events of the baby hidden in the bulrushes, then rescued by Pharaoh's daughter. In spite of the benefits of royal education, wealth and training, the day came when Moses chose to be identified with God rather than enjoy these earthly privileges. He later killed an Egyptian slavemaster, was viciously rejected by his own people,

and ran for his life to the back side of the Midian desert. For forty years he herd-
ed sheep, knowing that he was a marked man for whom death was certain should
he return to Egypt. God responded that those who sought Moses' life were now
dead. Moses' past was unimportant in relation to his present and future fulfillment of God's purpose.

Second, Moses knew his **position** was inadequate. Moses was a shepherd, a man
without standing even with his own people. Pharaoh was the most powerful man
in Egypt, possibly in the entire world. Egyptians believed that the Pharaoh was
an actual descendent of a god. Pharaoh would never acknowledge Moses as the
representative of Israel's God, Jehovah. Of greater challenge to Moses was the
response of his own people. What right did he have to return claiming to be their
leader? To both audiences Moses was to proclaim that "I AM THAT I AM—THE
ONE TRUE GOD, TOTALLY SELF-EXISTENT" was the authority and power behind
his leadership. To validate His call, God gave Moses the ability to work miracles.

Finally, Moses believed his **person** was inadequate; in particular, his speaking
abilities. As an isolated sheepherder for 40 years, he lacked the polished speaking style of a statesman. He described himself as "slow of speech." Perhaps he
was a stutterer or suffered some other speech related disability. In response, God
reminded him that He had made Moses' mouth and would give him the right
words to say. To further allay his fears, God agreed to send his brother Aaron as
his temporary "mouthpiece."

In spite of God's answers to Moses' objections, like little Jimmy, Moses' feet were
cemented to the ground. He was so afraid of what was about to happen that he
couldn't move. But little Jimmy's story is also very similar to what happened next
to Moses. When Jimmy heard his father's voice, he had the courage to jump into
the firemen's net.

God had uniquely planned the course of Moses' life. He had protected him from
death as an infant. He had provided keen insight and knowledge of Pharaoh's
household and the governance of Egypt. He had placed within Moses a heart for
God and his people. The Midian desert proved to be a testing ground for Moses'
faithfulness, as well as providing intimate knowledge of the land on which his

people would journey. Even the 40 years of watching sheep prepared Moses for leading more than two million slaves to freedom in the Promised Land. When Moses began to listen to his Father's voice, he gained the assurance and confidence needed to accomplish the task God had called him to do.

Everyone feels inadequate at one time or another. Most people feel inadequate because they play the "Comparison Game." They look at what others have, how others dress and act, or at their talents. The more they compare themselves to others, the more inadequate they feel.

Do you know what happens next? After we compare ourselves with others and identify our so-called inadequacies, we start playing a new game called the "Pretender Game." Now we try to pretend to be someone we are not in order to cover up our inadequacies. The following funny story illustrates the dangers of playing a "Pretender Game."

A number of years ago, a large church was performing its annual Easter program—a very elaborate production with hundreds of actors, actresses and live animals. The climax occurred when the actor playing Jesus ascended heavenward amidst swelling anthems of choral music. During one performance, the play proceeded as planned until it was time for the crucifixion scene. The Roman soldier, using a real spear, was to pierce Jesus' side—pretend, of course. The soldier missed his mark and actually put a small wound into the actor's side. They continued as if nothing had happened. But when "Jesus" was taken from the cross, the fake blood included real blood from the actor. He was immediately taken to the hospital.

Now, consider the dilemma. "Jesus" was on his way to the hospital without having completed the scenes for the resurrection and ascension into Heaven. Fortunately, the producers of the program had a "back-up Jesus." He took his position and performed the resurrection scene. No one in the audience knew that this actor was the "back-up Jesus." No one knew, that is, until it was time for the ascension scene.

The "back-up Jesus" was almost 50 pounds lighter than the first "Jesus." No one had thought to readjust the weights on the pulleys to compensate for the lighter "Jesus." As a result, the "back-up Jesus" shot straight upward, hitting his head on a ceiling beam. He was knocked unconscious! Imagine the conversations at the hospital when the "back-up Jesus" was also brought in for emergency treatment.

Of course, the audience was unaware of all the mishaps or that the second "Jesus" had pretended to be the first "Jesus." The lesson from this story is very simple: There always comes a defining moment when the pretender is revealed for who he really is.

By now, you have probably identified an inadequacy you believe you have in your life. Consider the following two questions:

- Is your inadequacy the result of comparing yourself to someone else?

- Are you pretending to be someone you're not in order to cover up this inadequacy?

As long as you compare yourself to the "things of this world," you will feel like you are inadequate. Moses was able to do great things because he overcame his inadequacies by placing his complete trust in God.

We are never able, in our own strength, to live victoriously. However, when we allow God to take total control of our lives, our feelings of inadequacy are overcome by the comfort and strength He gives us. This is what happened in Moses' life. It can happen in your life.

> *"The Lord is my strength and my shield; my heart*
> *trusted in Him, and I am helped; therefore my heart*
> *greatly rejoices, and with my song I will praise Him."*
> *(Psalm 28:7)*

INQUIRY-ACTION 25.1

THE LIFE OF MOSES

List the five most significant events in the life of Moses.

1

2

3

4

5

INQUIRY-ACTION 25.2

THE LIFE OF MOSES

List the five most important lessons for life you have learned from your study of Moses.

1 _____

_____

_____

2 _____

_____

3 _____

_____

_____

4 _____

_____

5 _____

_____

INQUIRY-ACTION 25.3

THE LIFE OF MOSES

List five principles on handling personal inadequacies illustrated in the life of Moses.

1 _____

_____

_____

2 _____

_____

_____

3 _____

_____

_____

4 _____

_____

_____

5 _____

_____

_____

INQUIRY-ACTION 25.4

THE PERSECUTED VS. THE PERSECUTORS

Lessons to Be Learned

INQUIRY-ACTION 25.5

2 CORINTHIANS 3:4–5

Use the words in the bank to write the verses.

adequacy	claim	have	sufficient
adequate	comes	in	that
and	competence	is	think
anything	competent	not	this
are	confidence	of	through
as	consider	our	toward
before	for	ours	to
being	from	ourselves	trust
but	God	such	we
Christ	God-ward	sufficiency	

JOB

Surviving Bad Things That Happen

It was a Sunday afternoon in October of 1997. Andre Thornton and his wife Gertrude packed for their last trip back to West Chester, Pennsylvania. Packing was not unusual for this family of four. As a minor and major league baseball player, Andre had moved his family many times. But this time was different. Andre had earned the starting position at first base for the Cleveland Indians, the place he hoped would be a permanent home. Having just bought a new house in Cleveland, they were going back to close out their apartment near Philadelphia.

Because the family liked to travel at night, their van came complete with beds for five-year-old Andy and two-year-old Theresa. The quiet hours of darkness allowed Andre time to think about the past year. His family was happy and the fans in Cleveland loved him. His health was great and his future was bright. His faith in the Lord had provided him with the strength to "keep on keeping on" when he was struggling in the minor league. He was so thankful for all that God had given to him.

Little did he know that his faith would soon be tested by the most difficult circumstances anyone could imagine. As he reached the higher elevations of the Pocono Mountains, he noticed that it was beginning to rain and that the temperature had dropped. He had lots of experience driving in that kind of weather, but would have to be careful of icy roads. Gradually the light snow and freezing rain worsened. He began to take extra precautions as he wove his way through the mountain passes. Suddenly, he felt the impact of a blast of wind hitting the side of his van and forcing him onto a slick, frozen shoulder. Immediately, Andre realized that the van was out of control. It was sliding sideways and there was no way he could stop it. The last sounds he heard were the screams of his family as the van struck the guard rail, overturned and hurtled down the mountain side.

When Andre regained consciousness, he realized the seriousness of the situation. While being treated in the hospital emergency room, he learned that young Andy was okay, but his wife and daughter had died instantly in the crash. Grief flooded his soul.

But, as he tells the story later, so did God's peace and the comfort of His Word. Although the pain was excruciating and interminable, his faith in the Lord provided the strength he needed to go on. He assures all who listen to his testimony that throughout this terrible experience, God never left him alone.

Tragedy and suffering are facts of life. Regardless of your age, your position in life or your wealth; you will eventually face difficulties that will challenge your faith in the Lord. Are you a "sunshine Christian" or one whose faith can withstand the trials of life? That is an important question for every believer to consider.

As you read the story about Andre Thornton, did a particular person in the Bible come to your mind—perhaps Job? Although far more severe, his story also recounts how an individual's faith was tested through tragedy and suffering. Actually, the story begins in Heaven where God reminds Satan that Job is "a blameless and upright man, one who fears God and shuns evil" (Job 1:8). Satan responds with a question to God that might be paraphrased: If you take away all of the good things Job has, will he be so blameless and upright?

God decides to prove Satan wrong by allowing him to remove Job's family, property and finally his health. God allows Satan to "destroy him (Job) without cause" (Job 2:3). While most people ask the question, "Can you trust God?', Satan's question to God was, "Can you trust a man?" God created mankind with freedom to choose; we are not merely puppets. In the crucible of suffering, will Job still choose to worship God? What a challenge!

Of course, Job is completely unaware of Satan's accusations in Heaven. All he knows is that in a very short time he loses his children, his wealth and now sits on an ash heap, scraping his painful open sores with a piece of broken pottery. For the next 36 chapters, Job has an ongoing dialog with his wife, three friends and a young stranger in an attempt to understand why all of these tragedies have occurred in his life. His wife believes that he should, "curse God and die." But Job refuses to "sin with his lips" (Job 2:9–10). Even while bemoaning his own birth, he confidently proclaims, "Though He slay me, yet will I trust Him" (Job 13:15).

Job's friends believe that he is not blameless and is suffering as a just punishment for terrible sins. However, Job defends his innocence, even calling upon God to be his witness. Suddenly God appears "out of the whirlwind" (Job 38:1) and displays His awesome nature through the creation and control of the universe. He also assures Job of His tender heartfelt care. The best answer to a hurting heart is to know more of the character of God. The psalmist said, "God has spoken once, twice I have heard this: That power belongs to God. Also to You, O Lord, belongs mercy" (62:11–12).

Job's profound faith in God's sovereignty and love gives him confidence to proclaim, "For I know that my Redeemer lives, and He shall stand at last on the earth. Whom I shall see for myself, and my eyes shall behold, and not another. How my heart yearns within me!" (Job 19:25, 27). In the end, God rewards his faithfulness with renewed health, a new family and a double portion of wealth.

The book of Job provides a very practical answer to an age-old question, "How do I survive the bad things that happen in my life?" It is important to remember that we don't always know why suffering and tragedy happen. Man can never know the mind or ways of God. Remember, God criticized Job for pretending to understand when it was impossible to know why he had experienced so much personal loss. So when bad things do happen in our lives, how should we respond? Job has some very important lessons for us.

First, when facing difficult times, remember who is in control of your life. Job knew that no matter what happened to him, God was in control. All that he had, including his life, belonged to God. As you know, the world's perspective is to achieve happiness through the things we have or the people we know. But what happens when we no longer have these things? Job reminds us that whether or not we understand the circumstances of life, true happiness can only come when we acknowledge God's complete control in our lives.

Second, when facing difficult times, don't focus on what's going on around you. It is one thing to admit that God is in control of your life. It is very different to completely trust God when tragedy strikes. Too often, when facing difficulties in our lives, we try to "work it out" on our own. We can never be successful in our own strength.

Third, when facing difficult times, testify to your faith in God's goodness. Job's wife wanted him to "curse God and die." Job refused. Instead, he praised God and renewed his faith in Him. Although Job could not understand why, his public declaration of faith made it very clear that he was not going to blame God for what had happened in his life.

Finally, when facing difficult times, don't be afraid to seek support from a friend. Job's friends did not encourage and support him during these difficult times. They used this time to accuse him and lecture him. It is important, throughout your life, to develop friendships with individuals who honor the Lord and will stand with you when bad things happen.

If you are experiencing difficult times in your life right now, take that first step and regain perspective. God knows what you are facing and is in complete control of the situation. Trust Him! He will use today's experiences to prepare you for tomorrow's victories.

INQUIRY-ACTION 26.1

FROM BAD TO WORSE

1. A servant arrives to say _____
_____ (Job 1:13–15).

But could things get worse?

2. A servant arrives to say _____
_____ (Job 1:16).

But could things get worse?

3. A servant arrives to say _____
_____ (Job 1:17).

But could things get worse?

4. A servant arrives to say _____
_____ (Job 1:18–19).

But what was Job's response?

5. He _____
_____
_____ (Job 1:20–22).

But could things get worse?

6. Satan _____
_____ (Job 2:7–8).

INQUIRY-ACTION 26.1 (CONTINUED)

But could things get worse?

7. Job's wife _____

_____ (Job 2:9).

But what was Job's response?

8. Job replied _____

_____ (Job 2:10–11).

But could things get worse?

9. Elephaz, Bildad, Zophar and Elihu insist that the reason for Job's trouble is _____

_____

(Job 4:7–8; 8:2–6; 11:14–15; 22:5 and 23; 36:11–12).

But what was God's position?

10. God stated that Job _____

_____ (Job 1:1).

How can a man be right with God?

11. Mankind must have _____

_____

_____ (Job 9:2, 32–33; 16:19–21; 1 John 2:1–2; Ephesians 2:13–14).

So what was Job's response?

12. Job said _____

_____

_____ (Job 13:15; 19:25–27).

INQUIRY-ACTION 26.1 (CONTINUED)

But could things get better?

13. From a whirlwind, God asked, "Where were you when . . .?"

- I formed the _____ (Job 38:4)?

- I strung the _____ (Job 38:7, 31–32)?

- I set the boundaries of the _____ (Job 38:8)?

- I separated _____ (Job 38:19)?

- I crafted _____ (Job 38:21, 29–30)?

- I directed _____ (Job 38:24, 34–35)?

- I established the ways of _____
    (Job 38:39–41:34)?

So, what is the nature of God?

14. God is _____

_____ (Job 5:9; 9:10; 11:7–8; 12:13).

But could things get better?

15. Job replied, _____

_____ (Job 42:2).

But could things get better?

16. The Lord _____

_____ (Job 42:10, 12–13).

INQUIRY-ACTION 26.2

WHY BAD THINGS HAPPEN TO GOOD PEOPLE

Reason 1: **The world is under the curse of sin.**

_____

_____

_____

_____

_____

_____

Reason 2: **There are natural consequences to wrong choices.**

_____

_____

_____

_____

_____

_____

Conclusions:

_____

_____

_____

_____

INQUIRY-ACTION 26.3

WHY BAD THINGS HAPPEN TO GOOD PEOPLE

Reason 3: **God is forming our character through . . .**

1) Pruning: _____

_____

2) Patience: _____

_____

3) Chastisement for sin: _____

4) Obedience: _____

5) Preparation for service: _____

Reason 4: **We are identified with Christ and His eternal purposes.** _____

_____

_____

Conclusions:

_____

_____

_____

INQUIRY-ACTION 26.4

A SUMMARY OF JOB'S ADVICE

Principle 1:   Remember who is in control.

Principle 2:   Don't focus on the circumstances around you.

Principle 3:   Testify to your faith.

Principle 4:   Seek support from family and friends.

INQUIRY-ACTION 26.5

JOB 19:25 AND 27

Complete the diagram of sentences in order to write the verses.

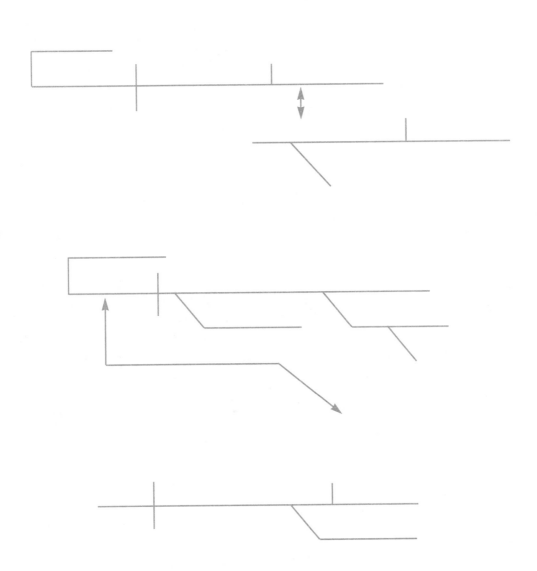

INQUIRY–ACTION 26.5 (CONTINUED)

JOHN

Surviving Loneliness

The walk home seemed a lot longer than it had the day before. It was over. Jason had not made the final cut for the freshman basketball team. There wouldn't be another chance, at least not this year. For the entire season he would be watching the games from the bleachers.

Being a part of the team had been one of the most important things in his life. Ever since sixth grade he had been playing basketball with the same group of guys. They did everything together. Now the guys would continue to do all the things they had done before—only without him. He had never felt so all alone in his entire life.

He should have seen it coming. When he was in the seventh grade, he was 5' 6" tall, the tallest guy on the team and the starting center. It was the greatest year of his life. It was the first year that all of the guys had played together as a team. He remembered the coach telling his dad that he had real potential. He knew that basketball was his game, and he couldn't wait until the next season.

During the eighth grade season, Jason was back on the team. However, he started at the forward position instead of at center. Although still one of the taller guys on the team, he hadn't grown at all. He was still 5' 6". Both he and the team played well, but Jason wished he could have played center just like he had the year before.

Things changed when he entered ninth grade. He knew there was a problem the very first day at school. To begin with, a lot of new students had transferred to the school. He would face stiffer competition during tryouts. But the biggest challenge was his height. While all of his teammates had continued to grow taller, Jason was still 5' 6". He had not grown, even a half inch, in over two years. He was now one of the shortest guys trying to make the freshman team.

It was close, but not close enough. He almost made the final cut. Actually, he was the last one to be cut. He couldn't believe that after two years, his basketball career was over. But it wasn't the game that he was really going to miss—it was his friends. Now he was "on the outside looking in." It was a lonely feeling.

Can you identify with the loneliness that Jason experienced? Maybe the reason for the loneliness you've faced had nothing to do with being on "the team." Loneliness can occur when moving to a new city or school, when there is a party and you're not invited, or no one wants to sit with you during lunch. Maybe you feel lonely even when you are in a crowd.

Sometimes feelings of loneliness are to be expected. For example, it is quite normal to feel "all alone" when attending a new school for the first time. A new schedule, unknown teachers and no friends can make anyone miss their former school. Whenever you are in a new situation, you wish you could go back to the "way it used to be."

The Apostle John must have felt this same sense of loneliness when he was exiled to the Isle of Patmos. For years he had faithfully ministered to the churches in Asia Minor. Not only did he have a close working relationship with the disciples, he also had made many friends in the churches throughout the region. His extensive writings, including the Gospel of John and 1, 2 and 3 John, were having a powerful impact upon believers. His ministry was very successful. However, it was because of his success that the Roman emperor Domitian had sent him to Patmos.

The emperor Domitian came to power in 81 A.D. at the age of 30. When he assumed power he was already an angry and bitter man. His father, Vespasian, and his older brother, Titus, had not trusted him. As a result, he was excluded from power during their reign. When he finally obtained the throne, he immediately set out to prove that he could also be a strong leader.

His rule soon became a "reign of terror." He became so fearful of conspiracies, that he trusted no one. Christians were his prime targets. John was just one of many who were persecuted, exiled or killed. Finally, in 96 A.D., Domitian's own wife helped to murder him.

While John lived on the island, he probably served as a slave in the quarries and mines. Most certainly, he suffered desolation and hardships. Historical writers report that John was released from exile after the death of Domitian and died sometime before 118 A.D. Being aged and feeble, John was carried on a cot by young men as he visited various Christian assemblies during the reign of Trajan. John's final years were characterized by the singular central message of his life, "Little children, love one another." The importance of this message expands when considering the lonely years John experienced separated from family and friends. Perhaps there were many occasions when John and others asked, "Why?"

But God had a plan. It was on the Isle of Patmos that God revealed to John the future of the earth and all of mankind. Through a vision, God detailed the specific events that would occur before the end of the world and the creation of a new heaven and a new earth. It became John's task to write about the vision God revealed to him. The loneliness that John experienced was overshadowed by the honor that God gave him. John's place of imprisonment and exile became the location that God chose for him to write the book of Revelation, the last book of our Bible.

Sometimes the loneliness we experience is not as dramatic as John's exile to the Isle of Patmos. Most of the time we are not banished to some barren island. However, loneliness always hurts. Although there are people all around, we can suffer from loneliness. The reasons are myriad.

- sensing that we don't fit in
- not having friends
- feeling that nobody cares
- lacking family members who provide emotional support
- not belonging to a youth group that encourages us spiritually
- not personally experiencing God's acceptance and direction for our lives
- seeming to be invisible

Do you sometimes feel that no one wants to talk with you, be seen with you, or even look at you? In the midst of so many people, are you alone? Don't panic! God knows all about the loneliness you face in your life. During times of solitude God can teach you some lessons that cannot be learned any other way. Some of these lessons include the following:

1) Learn to depend on God alone. No matter how lonely you feel right now, if you have accepted Jesus Christ as your Savior, you are never alone. The Lord promised His followers, "I will never leave you or forsake you" (Hebrews 13:5). That's a promise that you can always count on. You can learn that Christ alone is sufficient for every need.

2) Learn to be comfortable with yourself. You can be your own best friend. It takes time to think about the person you are and the person you want to become. Some people are so busy that they never have time for themselves. Learn to appreciate the quiet times of solitude as opportunities to better know yourself. "I will bless the Lord who has given me counsel; my heart also instructs me in the night seasons. I have set the Lord always before me; because He is at my right hand I shall not be moved. Therefore my heart is glad, and my glory rejoices; my flesh will also rest in hope" (Psalm 16:7–9).

3) Learn to treasure the relationships you have with others. Building friendships with family and friends is an important part of life. Experiencing loneliness can help you understand this need. The Lord can then lead you in effectively developing these relationships. "By this all will know that you are My disciples, if you have love for one another" (John 13:35).

INQUIRY–ACTION 27.1

EIGHT IMPORTANT FACTS ABOUT JOHN

1

2

3

4

5

6

7

8

INQUIRY-ACTION 27.2

REFLECTIONS ON LONELINESS

1. What is the most important personal lesson you have learned this week?

_____

_____

_____

_____

2. What do you believe you need to do to "reach out" to someone who is lonely?

_____

_____

_____

_____

3. What will you do the next time you experience loneliness?

_____

_____

_____

_____

A Friend Is . . .

INQUIRY–ACTION 27.3 (CONTINUED)

INQUIRY–ACTION 27.3 (CONTINUED)

INQUIRY-ACTION 27.3 (CONTINUED)

INQUIRY-ACTION 27.4

1 JOHN 4:21–5:2

+ → 1/2 – f + v ↓

:

t +

– a + u

   2 b +

? ?

•

t +  = → + st =

,

↓ +

  +  2

– a

Inquiry-Action 27.4 (CONTINUED)

= (bee) + (goat) **− a + n** ↓ (temple)

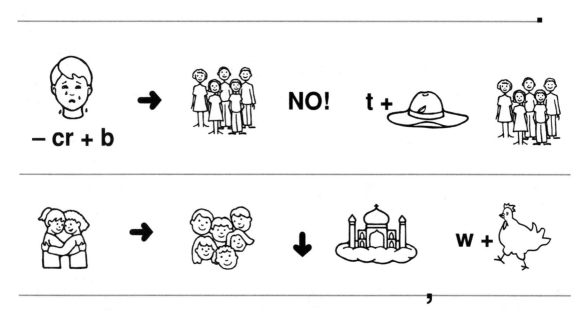

− cr + b → (people) **NO!** **t +** (hat) (people)

→ ↓ **w +** (chicken) **,**

(people) (couple) (temple) **+** (key) **+ p** (temple)

.

OTHNIEL

Surviving a Poor Background

Most men own at least one suit. Depending on their profession, they may own many more. However, there are special occasions when a suit is needed. That is why most men have at least one.

The story is told of a minister who was in need of a dark color suit to wear at a funeral he had been asked to conduct. He had just accepted his first position as pastor of a small, rural church. Although he did have one suit, it was not the right color. Another problem was that he had very little money.

So he went to the local pawn shop. He had been told that they had the best prices in town on everything. Although there were not many suits on the rack, he was able to find exactly what he needed. The black suit was just the right size and very inexpensive. He couldn't believe his good fortune. It was more than he could have asked for.

As he took out his wallet to pay for the suit, he was curious as to why the suit was so cheap. The pawnbroker didn't want to answer; he hesitated at first. But, realizing that it was important to be honest with the young minister, he admitted that many of their black suits had been owned by the local mortuary. These suits had been used on deceased bodies for viewing and then removed before burial.

The young minister was visibly startled. He questioned himself, "Do I want to wear a suit that was worn by a dead man?" But it was a good buy. He clearly couldn't afford to pay any more. So he bought the suit and left the store.

He couldn't seem to shake the thought that he was wearing a suit that had been on a man lying in a coffin. But it calmed his concerns when he realized that no one else would ever know. All he had to do was act normal.

Everything was fine until he was in the middle of his sermon and casually started to stick his hand into the pocket of the pants. All of a sudden, he knew why the suit was so cheap. THERE WERE NO POCKETS IN THE PANTS! Then he realized why there were no pockets. Dead men can't take anything with them when they die. Talk about an unforgettable object lesson. He preached a great sermon about the importance of eternity while wearing a suit that had been on a corpse. Again and again, he drove home the point: Dead men don't need pockets.

Dead men don't need pockets. That important message was taught by Jesus in Luke 12:16–21.

> *"Then he spoke a parable to them, saying: "The ground of a certain rich man yielded plentifully. And he thought within himself, saying, 'What shall I do, since I have no room to store my crops?' So he said, 'I will do this: I will pull down my barns and build greater, and there I will store all my crops and my goods. And I will say to my soul, 'Soul, you have many goods laid up for many years; take your ease; eat, drink, and be merry.' But God said to him, 'Fool! This night your soul will be required of you; then whose will those things be which you have provided?' So is he who lays up treasure for himself and is not rich toward God."*

The riches of this world are of little importance in light of eternity. In this parable the Lord reminds us that it is our relationship with Him that must be our greatest concern. Whether we are rich or poor, there is nothing in this world that is of eternal value.

Just as there are many who come from a wealthy background, there are also those who come from a poor background. Those who have little money or possessions are just as likely to be tempted by "the things of this world" as anyone else. Surviving a poor background begins with our minds. Proverbs 23:7 says it this way: "For as he thinks in his heart, so is he." If our minds are focused on our personal problems, rather than on the Lord, we will never be victorious.

Othniel's background did not prevent him from accepting Caleb's challenge recorded in Joshua 15:16. Caleb had just defeated the Anakim in the area surrounding the city of Debir. Caleb asked for a volunteer to lead his army against the Anakim in Debir. Othniel stepped forward to lead the troops.

Othniel could have easily left the task to someone else. He was young, he lacked experience and he did not come from a wealthy or influential family. It could easily be said that Othniel was a "nobody." But he purposed in his mind to not allow his circumstances or background to get in the way of doing God's Will.

In spite of his poor background, God gave him the victory. Because of his military victories, he won the hand of Caleb's daughter in marriage. Together they inherited some very valuable land containing natural springs that were extremely important in the dry, parched desert. Later Othniel became the first judge of Israel whom the "Spirit of the Lord came on" to deliver God's people and to bring 40 years of peace to the nation.

Have you ever thought of yourself as a "nobody"? Many young people do. Some see themselves as nobodies because they believe they lack athletic or musical talents. Others see themselves as nobodies because they don't believe that they are important to anyone. And still others see themselves as nobodies because they don't have the money or possessions that others have. Othniel could have easily had these same kinds of thoughts. It is likely that Kenaz, Othniel's father, died during the 38 years of wandering in the wilderness. As an orphan he had limited wealth and few rights. Yet somewhere, within the depths of his own heart, lay the courage to step forward and achieve victory.

Surviving a difficult background begins with an understanding of what is of greatest importance. Paul reminds us that whatever our circumstances, we must learn to be content (Philippians 4:11). Again, in 1 Timothy 6:6, he provides the formula for true wealth: "But godliness with contentment is great gain." Based on this verse, the formula would be:

Godliness + Contentment → Great Gain

Godliness refers to a sincere desire to walk according to the principles of God's Word. In Psalm 119:10–11 David says, "With my whole heart I have sought you:

Oh, let me not wander from Your commandments! Your word I have hidden in my heart, that I might not sin against You." God has given us His Word as our guide. It is up to us to choose to follow its teaching.

Contentment refers to a peace and satisfaction that comes when you accept what God has given to you. For some people, this will be the hardest part of the formula to follow. This means that you are willing to be satisfied even if you don't have the money or possessions that you want. This means you do not fret if your background is less than ideal. Contentment is the ability to say to God, "Lord, I am thankful for who I am and what I have."

Great gain refers to true wealth. Look again at the parable in Luke 12. The rich man had many possessions and great wealth. He was making plans to build even bigger barns so that he could store up greater riches. But then his life came to a sudden end. Like the suit with no pockets, he could not take any of this wealth with him. All of this wealth would stay behind. As Jesus explained in verse 21, the man was "not rich toward God."

Although having money is not a sin, it is not the wealth of this world that should consume us. Neither should having a certain family name or popularity based on looks or abilities. Regardless of our backgrounds, we have enormous value to God.

- We bear God's image.
- We become God's children through Christ.
- We are loved as the "apple of His eye" and "cherished treasure."
- We are God's channel of blessing to the world.
- We have an eternal home in Heaven.

Therefore, we should desire to be "rich toward God." True wealth is obediently following God's Word (godliness) and being satisfied with who you are and what God has given to you (contentment). This is the formula for surviving a poor background.

Inquiry-Action 28.1

BACKGROUND CHECK

denied the Lord

was an orphan

was young, timid and sickly

was a cripple

were rough, uneducated
    fishermen

married a harlot

suffered a terrible illness

grandfather and father were
    murderers

became discouraged and quit

father killed himself

was a slave

great-great grandmother was a
    destitute widow

was not beautiful in appearance

was a poor shepherd exiled to a
    desert

mother tried to kill him

parent was poor and of low social
    status

Moses *(Exodus 3:1)*

Hosea *(1:2–3; 2:19–20)*

David *(Ruth 4:21–22)*

Jesus *(Luke 2:22–24)*

Timothy *(4:12; 5:23)*

John Mark *(Acts 15:36–40;*
    2 Timothy 4:11)

Mephibosheth *(2 Samuel 4:4)*

Joash *(2 Kings 11:1–2; 22:1–2)*

Esther *(2:7)*

Onesimus *(Philemon 10, 16)*

Jonathan *(1 Samuel 31:4)*

James and John *(Matthew*
    4:20–21)

Peter *(Matthew 26)*

Josiah *(2 Kings 21:16, 19–22, 24)*

Leah *(Genesis 29:16–17)*

Hezekiah *(2 Kings 20:1–6)*

INQUIRY-ACTION 28.2

OTHNIEL'S TWO STORIES

Story 1

Othniel's Age: _____

The Situation: _____

_____

The Victory: _____

_____

The Result: _____

_____

Story 2

Othniel's Age: _____

The Situation: _____

_____

The Victory: _____

_____

The Result: _____

_____

INQUIRY-ACTION 28.2 (CONTINUED)

Lessons to Be Learned:

1. _____

_____

2. _____

_____

3. _____

_____

Othniel's Character:

Courageous: _____

_____

Capable: _____

_____

Humble: _____

_____

Godly: _____

_____

An Important Application to My Life:

_____

_____

_____

INQUIRY-ACTION 28.3

JESUS' TEACHING ABOUT MONEY

Look up each of the following four verses. Then note the warning Jesus gave us from each verse. After you have identified the warning, write a one-to-two sentence application of that warning to your life.

Mark 4:19

Warning: _____

Application: _____

_____

_____

Luke 12:15

Warning: _____

Application: _____

_____

_____

Luke 12:34

Warning: _____

Application: _____

_____

_____

Matthew 6:24

Warning: _____

Application: _____

_____

_____

INQUIRY-ACTION 28.4

JEREMIAH 29:11–13

A	B	C	D	E	F	G	H	I	J	K	L	M
✡	❖	✝	♣	✿	◆	◇	★	☆	◉	✩	✰	✖

N	O	P	Q	R	S	T	U	V	W	X	Y	Z
▲	✚	○	✳	✴	✳	♥	▼	✦	■	✺	✸	✺

NOAH

Surviving Ridicule and Vengeance

Jeremy's birth would not be an easy one. For weeks his mother had known that there were problems with her baby. The doctors were not quite sure of the extent of his problems, but they were expecting the worst. They knew the delivery would be difficult. Jeremy had been given less than a 50–50 chance of surviving.

It was hard and it was long, but Jeremy survived. Even from his outward appearance, the doctor and nurses knew that things were not right. As soon as he was stable, the testing began. For the first three weeks of Jeremy's life, all he knew was the pain associated with test after test after test.

Finally, the verdict was in. In addition to a serious heart problem, Jeremy's ability to grow was severely handicapped. The doctor used a long, complicated medical term to describe the condition. But Jeremy's parents didn't really care what it was called. All they knew was that their son would probably not grow more than three feet tall and was not expected to live to adulthood.

The years passed and soon it was time for Jeremy to start school. He was looking forward to a new beginning. His early childhood had not been a pleasant one. In addition to being sick most of the time, he didn't really have any friends. He was often mocked and ridiculed because of the way he looked, but he just knew that he would be able to make new friends at school.

It was the night before the first day of school that "it" actually happened for the first time. That night, Jeremy sensed that God had a very important purpose for his life. He knew that he would never be like the other children. He also knew that he would not live to be very old. But, most importantly, he now knew that God had placed him on this earth for a purpose. Although this was the first time Jeremy had felt this way, it would not be the last. God had him here for a reason. He was convinced of it!

The first day in school did not go as Jeremy had hoped. The other students stared at him, laughed at him and called him names. It was a humiliating experience. He wanted to go home, but he knew he couldn't. Day after day, the children either mocked him or ignored him. There were times when Jeremy was so angry that all he wanted to do was fight back. But he knew better. Between his size and his health, he wouldn't stand a chance.

The years passed. Although the ridicule continued, it didn't seem to bother Jeremy as much any more. Maybe the other students had decided to treat him with more respect. Then again, maybe he was just getting used to it. However, the one thing that he did know for certain was that God had a very special plan for him. Ever since that night before the first day of school, he had become convinced that God had a purpose. He never wavered in his belief.

It was time once again for the annual school picnic. Jeremy always looked forward to this day. Even though the students still ignored him, it did seem like they were friendlier to him than on a normal school day. It was a day when even the "big kids" treated the younger ones with respect.

All of a sudden he saw a group of students and adults run past him toward a construction area near the road. From the bits and pieces of frantic conversation that he heard, he knew that one of the first-graders was in trouble. His short body prevented him from running like the rest of the children. As a result, a large crowd had already gathered by the time he got to the accident site. But this time, his size was to his advantage. He easily worked his way to the front.

"She's down there," someone screamed, pointing into a hole that couldn't be more than 18 inches in diameter. The little girl had fallen about 20 feet into the hole and was wedged in tightly. Although a rope had been lowered down to her, no one could convince her to grab hold of it. She was scared to death.

Jeremy stepped forward. "Tie the rope around me," he said. "I can fit into the hole. Lower me down and I will get her." No one said a word. One of the teachers tied the rope around Jeremy while two others prepared to lower him into the hole. The crowd had calmed down. Jeremy had clearly taken control of the situation.

It was only a matter of minutes before Jeremy and the little girl emerged from the hole, but it seemed like an eternity. The cheers from the crowd, and the hugs that Jeremy received, were more than he had ever expected. For the rest of the day, no one could stop talking about Jeremy's bravery.

Jeremy never saw the end of that school year. His health problems worsened and he had to enter the hospital in April. A few days later, he passed away. His memory is still alive at the school. Although ridiculed and mocked by the other students, Jeremy knew that God had him on this earth for a reason. No one would ever forget who he was, or what he did.

No one likes to be made fun of. Although the pain of being mocked and ridiculed is not always evident on the outside, the hurt inside is real. If you have ever been the object of ridicule, you know the feeling. You probably have a very clear understanding of what Jeremy was experiencing.

Can you imagine the ridicule that Noah must have faced? Noah devoted 120 years of his life to constructing the Ark. Think about the questions he must have been asked during those years.

Neighbor 1: "Who told you to build a boat that big?"

Noah: "God."

Neighbor 2: "But there's no water around deep enough for your boat. Where's the water going to come from?"

Noah: "God is going to send a great flood that will cover all of the earth."

Neighbor 3:   "Why do you have to make the boat so big?"

Noah: "God told me that it had to be large enough to hold two of every kind of animal and bird."

Neighbor 4:   "So, Noah, you say there is going to be a worldwide flood and this boat is going to keep you and two of every animal in the world safe? You've been in the sun too long; your brain is fried. I think you need to see a doctor. NOW!"

Maybe this is not quite the way that the conversation went. But there were questions. Lots of them! And there was certainly laughter, mockery and ridicule directed at Noah and his "super-boat."

But Noah knew that God had him on this earth for a reason. Even though, at times, the ridicule and the unbelief angered him, he still had a task to do. He had to look beyond the mocking words and his personal feelings. God was at work. He had been chosen to be a part of God's plan.

Pretend that you were there at that precise moment when Noah finished building the Ark. As he looks upon his finished work, you ask him, "Noah, how were you able to survive the ridicule and the mockery for all of these years?"

"It's not hard," he responds. "First, you have to evaluate the reason for the ridicule. If you're being mocked for doing what God has commanded you to do, then you can't let it bother you. Second, faithfully complete God's business in a way that honors Him. Don't let the ridicule cause you to say or do something you shouldn't. Finally, trust God to keep His Word. He has a plan for our lives. Don't give up on Him. He will never give up on you."

That's good advice!

INQUIRY–ACTION 29.1

LESSONS FROM THE LIFE OF NOAH

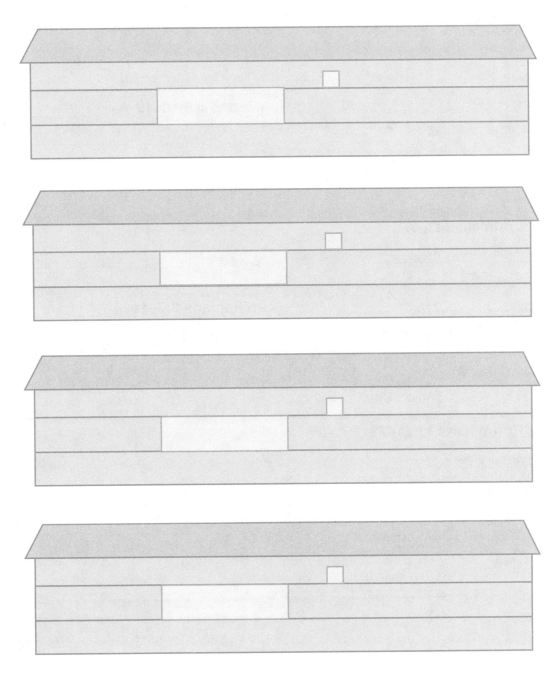

INQUIRY-ACTION 29.2

PERSECUTED FOR RIGHTEOUSNESS

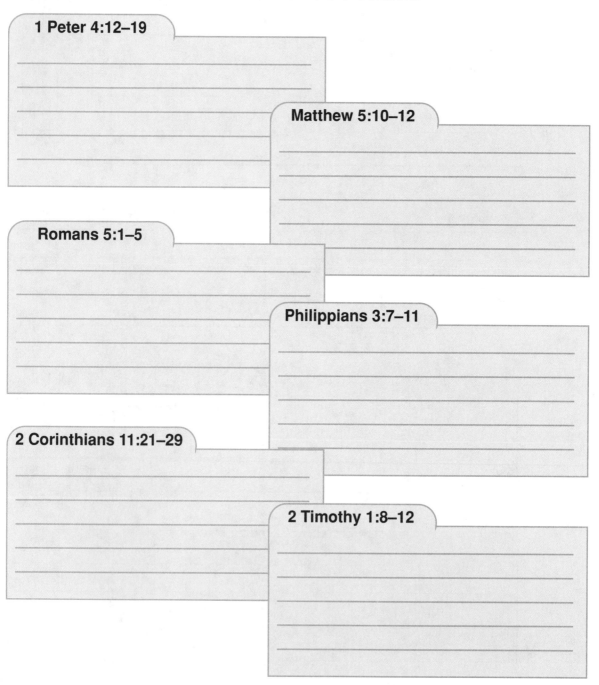

1 Peter 4:12–19

Matthew 5:10–12

Romans 5:1–5

Philippians 3:7–11

2 Corinthians 11:21–29

2 Timothy 1:8–12

INQUIRY-ACTION 29.3

REAPING RIDICULE

Some Lessons I've Learned about Taming My Tongue

1

2

3

4

My promise to myself is . . .

INQUIRY-ACTION 29.4

MATTHEW 5:10–12

1 Blessed are those who _____ persecuted for righteous-

ness' sake, _____ theirs is the kingdom _____ heaven.

Blessed are you _____ they revile and persecute

_____, and say all kinds _____ evil against you falsely

_____ My sake. Rejoice and _____ exceedingly glad,

for great _____ your reward in heaven, _____ so they

persecuted the _____ who were before you.

2 Blessed are those _____ are persecuted for _____

sake, for theirs _____ the kingdom of _____. Blessed

are you _____ they revile and _____ you, and say

_____ kinds of evil _____ you falsely for _____

sake. Rejoice and _____ exceedingly glad, for _____ is

your reward _____ heaven, for so _____ persecuted

the prophets _____ were before you.

INQUIRY-ACTION 29.4 (CONTINUED)

3 Blessed are _____ who are _____ for

righteousness' _____ for theirs _____ the kingdom

_____ heaven. Blessed _____ you when _____

revile and _____ you, and _____ all kinds _____

evil against _____ falsely for _____ sake. Rejoice

_____ be exceedingly _____ for great _____

your reward _____ heaven, for _____ they

persecuted _____ prophets who _____ before you.

4 Blessed _____ those _____ are _____ for

_____ sake, _____ theirs _____ the _____

of _____ Blessed _____ you _____ they

_____ and _____ you, _____ say _____

kinds _____ evil _____ you _____ for

_____ sake. _____ and _____ exceedingly

_____ for _____ is _____ reward _____

heaven, _____ so _____ persecuted _____

prophets _____ were _____ you.

INQUIRY-ACTION 29.4 (CONTINUED)

5

SOLOMON

Surviving Unfulfilled Dreams

"I wish that I could . . . ." Have you ever wished for something? If you have, you know the excitement of having that wish come true. You also know the disappointment when it doesn't.

At a very young age, Jeff learned the disappointment of unfulfilled dreams. Although Jeff was from a very loving and happy family, they had little money. He was the youngest of five children from an old neighborhood on the outskirts of Knoxville.

There were two very special times of the year for Jeff: his birthday and Christmas. As his birthday approached, he began to drop hints on how great it would be to get a new basketball. He had just entered the 8th grade that year and had made the basketball team. He wanted a ball of his own so he could practice at home.

Jeff took every possible step to ensure that he would get that basketball. He did his chores without being asked. He volunteered to help his brothers and sisters with their work around the house. He even asked if he could wash the dog! All the time, Jeff continued to remind his parents about the basketball that he wanted.

His birthday finally arrived. After dinner, everyone gathered around the table to share birthday cake and to watch Jeff open his gifts. Immediately, Jeff saw the box he wanted to open first. It wasn't your typical box; it was the perfect shape for a basketball.

He took the box and tore off the bow and ribbon. Within seconds the wrapping paper had been discarded and he was pulling open the top to the box. He couldn't believe his eyes—the box contained a globe. Jeff's weakness in world geography had caught his parents' attention. They knew that their son needed a globe more than a basketball. Jeff faced the disappointment of an unfulfilled dream.

Our hopes and dreams are often centered around more than just possessions. That was certainly true in Rhonda's case. She was twelve years old when she first realized that, compared to the other girls in her class, she was skinny and unshapely. When she looked in the mirror, she felt that she was unattractive. Something had to be done.

Rhonda went to the local book store in search of an answer. It wasn't long before her eyes spied the solution on the cover of a glossy magazine. The advertisements promised that whoever followed this secret exercise program would develop the strength and figure of a world-class gymnast. The exercise program was just what Rhonda wanted. After nearly two weeks of anxious anticipation, video arrived in the mail. The next morning, Rhonda got up at 6:00 A.M. for her workout. According to the advertisements, she would see results in just two weeks.

On day eleven, as Rhonda was completing her routine, she seriously sprained her neck. After an early morning trip to the Emergency Room, she emerged with a neck brace. For the rest of the summer, she had to wear that brace. Restricted from physical activities, she lost contact with her classmates. No one seemed to want to be around a skinny kid in a neck brace—not at this age. Rhonda faced the disappointment of an unfulfilled dream.

Many times what begins as a "great expectation" ends up as a "great disappointment." Solomon surely began his life with great expectations. To begin with, he was the son of a king. His father, King David, had already made available to him all of the opportunities that a young man could ask for. Solomon had it all: the best possible education, travel throughout the known world and meeting the most powerful and brilliant people of his time.

In addition to the opportunities, Solomon was given the kingdom. For years his father David had fought to establish peace in Israel. Now, at the close of his life, the nation was free from outside invaders. There was no war on the horizon. As the mantle of leadership passed from David to Solomon, the dreams of the young king could soon become reality.

Solomon's greatness became known throughout the world. His wisdom was legendary. Leaders and wise men would come to him to settle disputes and obtain advice. In a short amount of time, he established a defense system unlike Israel had ever known. He had thousands of chariots and horsemen stationed in cities throughout Israel's countryside. Solomon's wealth was so great that it was impossible to know the total amount of riches he possessed. Solomon was both a builder and a writer. Under his direction, many elaborate buildings were constructed. Of course, the most famous was the Temple; even more elaborate was his king's palace. As a writer, Solomon produced some of the finest wisdom and dramatic literature the world had known. Inspired by God, the books of Proverbs, Ecclesiastes and the Song of Solomon are available to us today.

It seemed as if all of Solomon's dreams were coming true. He looked forward to that time when he could pass this vast and wealthy kingdom on to his son, as his father David had done for him. But that dream would go unfulfilled. Solomon made a tragic mistake.

His mistake is identified in the opening words of 1 Kings 11: "But King Solomon loved many foreign women . . . ." As was typical in the Old Testament, Solomon sealed many of the treaties he made with foreign rulers by marrying a member of their royal family. This was a dual violation of God's Law, which forbade marriage to foreign women and also decreed that a king of God's people must not have multiple wives. According to verse three, Solomon had a total of 1000 wives and concubines.

As a result, Solomon's heart turned away from God. At the beginning of his reign, Solomon faithfully worshiped the God of Israel. As he approached the end of his life, he had married so many wives, who worshiped pagan deities, that he no longer cared about the God of his father David.

As a result of Solomon's disobedience, the nation of Israel would be divided after his death. The wealthy, peaceful united kingdom that Solomon had worked so hard to establish would be taken from him. Although it would not happen during his lifetime, God told him that it would happen during the rule of his son, Rehoboam. Solomon experienced the disappointment of unfulfilled dreams.

Surely, you have experienced the agony of an unfulfilled dream. Like Jeff, maybe you didn't receive a special gift that you had been wanting for a long time. Although you may not share Rhonda's problem, maybe your lack of physical ability or good looks has prevented you from making the team or being popular with others. Everyone knows what it is like to have hopes and dreams that never come true.

If you stop and think about it, most of our hopes and dreams have to do with the "here and now." No wonder we experience disappointment when our dreams fail to materialize. When our focus is totally directed "inward," we are feeding our selfish desires. This was certainly true for Solomon. He married the wives from these pagan countries because he wanted to secure more wealth and power.

Solomon's focus upon dreams rooted in the "here and now" prevented him from honoring God. As a result, he did not make decisions with "eternity in view." In the end, all of the earthly wealth and power that he had gained was lost. The lesson for each of us is simple. When personal dreams go unfulfilled, consider whether or not these dreams have an "eternal perspective." Are they dreams characterized by greed, self or personal gain? Are they dreams based on wrong values? Are your hopes motivated by false expectations for the future? If so, this is why they may go unfulfilled. It is quite possible that the fulfillment of these dreams will cause you to turn your eyes and mind away from what is really important.

The closing comments of Solomon's life show that he had finally found the only true satisfaction in life:

> *"Let us hear the conclusion of the whole matter: Fear God and keep His commandments, for this is man's all." (Ecclesiastes 12:13)*

God alone is the fulfiller of hopes and dreams based in Him.

> *"Delight yourself also in the Lord, and He shall give you the desires of your heart." (Psalm 37:4)*

> *"Whom have I in heaven but You? And there is none upon earth that I desire besides You." (Psalm 73:25)*

> *"May He grant you according to your heart's desire, and fulfill all your purpose." (Psalm 20:4)*

INQUIRY-ACTION 30.1

Write the name of the building at the top of your ladder of success. What things must you pack into your backpack to achieve this success?

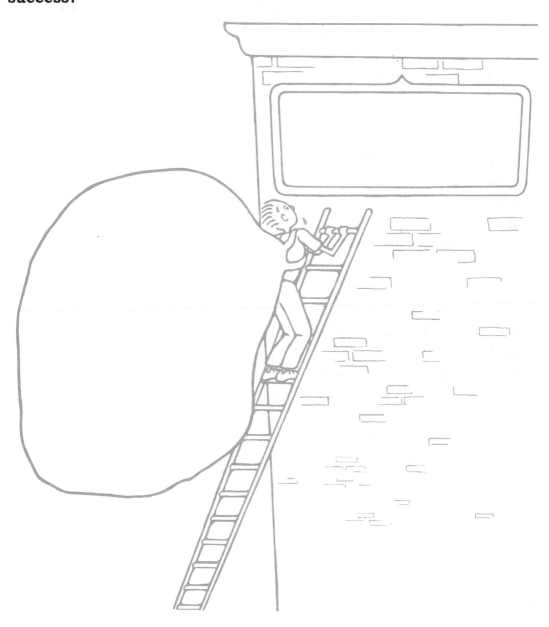

INQUIRY-ACTION 30.2

Solomon's Privileges	Solomon's Conclusions
1. Solomon was born to parents who loved him and ensured he had the finest background possible. He inherited the kingdom and had every opportunity for success.	Ecclesiastes 2:10–11
2. Solomon had extreme intelligence. Even more, he asked God for wisdom and discernment.	Ecclesiastes 1:16–18
3. Solomon had wealth and possessions beyond calculation.	Ecclesiastes 2:4–11
4. Solomon built the Temple and other great architectural wonders of the world. He was talented in many fields, especially writing.	Ecclesiastes 2:17–23
5. Solomon was famous throughout the world for his wisdom and wealth. He had many admirers but few friends.	Ecclesiastes 8:7–10
6. Solomon ruled over a peaceful, prosperous kingdom that had many alliances with other nations. His sin was disobedience as he married many wives, who turned his heart from God.	Ecclesiastes 2:1–3 and 9:3–10

INQUIRY–ACTION 30.2 (CONTINUED)

Solomon's Advice	Solomon's Lessons to Me
Proverbs 3:5–6	1.
Proverbs 1:7–8 and 2:9–11	2.
Proverbs 3:9–10, 21:21 and 22:4	3.
Proverbs 8:30–9:1 and 24:3–4	4.
Proverbs 17:17, 28:6–7 and 18:24	5.
Proverbs 7:1–3 and 21:2–3	6.

INQUIRY-ACTION 30.3

ECCLESIASTES 12:1A, 13–14

Use the definitions to help you write the verses.

bring to mind	_____	belonging to Jehovah	_____
this moment	_____	orders, laws	_____
belonging to you	_____	because	_____
the Maker of the universe	_____	pronoun-nonspecific thing	_____
not out	_____	equals	_____
determiner	_____	human being's	_____
Monday, Tuesday, . . .	_____	everything	_____
preposition = connected to	_____	because	_____
belonging to you	_____	Jehovah	_____
early years	_____	shall	_____
permit	_____	carry forth	_____
you and me	_____	each	_____
listen to	_____	achievement, doing	_____
determiner	_____	not out of	_____
end summary	_____	court decision	_____
preposition = connected to	_____	involving	_____
determiner	_____	each	_____
complete, all of the	_____	untold	_____
issue, belief	_____	item	_____
respect	_____	no mattering if	_____
Jehovah	_____	right, beneficial	_____
plus	_____	opposite to	_____
obey	_____	unrighteous, bad	_____

DANIEL

Surviving False Accusations

Sherry wanted to be the senior class president more than anything else in the world. She could only imagine how great it would be to stand before all of her classmates at the end of the year and deliver the final address to the graduating class. All eyes would be upon her. Everyone would intently listen to her words of wisdom. Her every move would be watched. If she could just win this election, she would be the center of attention for her entire senior year.

However, there was one slight problem—a student named Cindee. Cindee was new to the school late last year. Although little was known about her past, she had made a lot of friends since her move. Matter of fact, Sherry couldn't think of anyone who didn't like Cindee. The election was sure to be a close one. Sherry knew that if she didn't do something quickly, Cindee would more than likely become the senior class president.

Sherry was not going to let that happen! Since she was the editor of the school newspaper, she decided to write a story about the new students in school. She called the student-editor at Cindee's former school to ask questions about her. Much to her dismay, Cindee had been an honor student, had participated in a number of sports, and had been an active member of her youth group at church. This wasn't the juicy gossip Sherry had hoped to hear.

Near the end of the telephone interview, the editor off-handedly mentioned a fight at one of the girl's soccer games that had gotten a lot of girls in trouble. Although Cindee was on the soccer team, there was no mention that she had been involved. Of course, Sherry wasn't about to ask for more details.

Within minutes, Sherry was on the telephone informing her friends of what she had learned. "It's because Cindee got in trouble at her school that her parents moved here," Sherry said with confidence. "I'll bet that the entire soccer team would have been put on probation if she had remained on the team. She probably left the school in disgrace."

It wasn't long before the accusation was spreading throughout the student body. The students could hardly believe what they were hearing. Unfortunately, everyone was listening to the accusation, but no one was willing to step forward and ask Cindee if the information was true. Sherry knew that public opinion was turning in her favor. The election was only a week away.

It was the weekend before when Cindee learned about the accusation. "That's totally false!" she responded. "I didn't even play that day; I had injured my ankle at practice and was sitting on the sidelines for the entire game. My father got a promotion with his company. That's why we moved."

The following week, Cindee's closest friends worked hard to get out the true story about why Cindee had changed schools. The accusation was shown to be false. The facts were made available for all those who wanted to hear them.

In Cindee's case, the false accusations had been refuted in time to prevent their affecting the outcome of the election. She was elected to serve as senior class president. However, in too many cases, false accusations are not revealed for what they are. As a result, people are hurt and lives are changed forever.

This week's title, "Surviving False Accusations," clearly focuses on a familiar problem to most of us—what it is like when you are wrongly accused. Experiencing a false accusation surely puts you in a "survival" mode. You begin doing everything that you can to counter the lies and reveal the truth. However, you feel that you are chasing feathers in the wind.

Why do people make false accusations? What should you do when false accusations are made against you? The familiar story of Daniel provides some of the answers to these questions. Before we even begin to read Chapter 6 of Daniel, we already know two important facts about him. He was second in command to King Darius, and he was hated by the other leaders in the kingdom. He was hated because he was a Jew, was a man of integrity, and the king trusted him in all things.

The worst part, for these leaders, was that they had to obey Daniel. In deep resentment, they began looking for ways to accuse Daniel, but were unsuccessful because he was so faithful in all that he did. Finally, they decided that the only way that they could bring an accusation was to use Daniel's faith in his God against him.

Their plan was both simple and deceptive. They would encourage the king to sign a decree that would make it illegal to worship any god or man, except the king, for 30 days. They knew that King Darius would see the proposal as their way of honoring him. However, they also knew that Daniel would not obey the decree. Knowing Daniel's faith and consistent testimony, they used King Darius' pride to lay a trap for Daniel.

In Daniel 6:13 the leaders came to the king to report that Daniel continued to pray three times a day to his God. Then they falsely accused Daniel of having no respect for the king or his decree. Immediately, the king realized the mistake he had made. He knew that he had been tricked. There was no question that Daniel respected the king and his laws. But there was also no question that Daniel would remain faithful to his God.

You are familiar with the events that followed. "Daniel in the Lions' Den" is a favorite story you have heard since childhood. No doubt you have studied lessons in the story about God's care and about standing for what you believe. In addition to these, there are a number of lessons you can learn about "why" and "how" false accusations are made.

A false accusation is typically made against someone for one of four reasons. Sometimes the accusation is made to divert attention from the one making the accusation. When a little child does something wrong, the youngster frequently looks for someone else to blame in order to shift the attention away from himself.

A second reason for a false accusation is that the person is simply repeating gossip, not knowing whether it is true or not.

A third reason false accusations are made is a little harder to understand. A person who has a low self-concept is threatened by the successes of others. Therefore, he tries to "cut them down to his size" by harsh criticisms, cynical "cuts" and false accusations. It's his effort to make himself look and feel better.

Finally, a false accusation is made because the one making the accusation is angry and is seeking revenge. This was the reason that the false accusation was made against Daniel. The leaders hated him because of his relationship with King Darius and his righteous testimony.

Take another close look at Chapter 6. There are a number of lessons we can learn from Daniel's experience about "how" false accusers bring their accusations. As you consider the following methods, reflect upon the story at the beginning of this chapter as well as Daniel's situation.

Method 1: False accusers create a situation in order to lay a trap. The leaders proposed a decree that they knew the king would sign and Daniel would have to disobey.

Method 2: False accusers turn friends against you. King Darius was Daniel's friend. The leaders tried to cause a division between them.

Method 3: False accusers mix lies with truth when they make their accusations. Daniel truly respected the king. However, he could not obey this law.

Method 4: False accusers often resort to name-calling. Note that the leaders called Daniel a "Jew." Jews were generally not liked among the nations because of their strong belief in God and because of their determination to be a nation.

Perhaps the most important lesson we can learn from Daniel is that a personal, godly testimony is the best protection against a false accusation. If you live honestly before others, it will be difficult for someone to make a false accusation against you that will be believed. Your good reputation will protect you. People who know you won't believe them.

But there may be times when even a good reputation is not enough. When that happens, you must maintain a right spirit and attitude. Speak the truth, and trust the Lord to use it to uncover the lies brought against you. Time will be your friend in proving the accusations false.

The writer of Proverbs 16:7 knew that, in the end, truth would prevail. "When a man's ways please the Lord, He makes even his enemies to be at peace with him." The Christian's responsibility is simple:

SPEAK the truth, LIVE the truth—START TODAY!

INQUIRY-ACTION 31.1

DANIEL AND HIS FRIENDS

Even as a young ▮▮▮▮▮▮, Daniel's appearance and character opened doors to a royal education. Daniel and his friends, ▮▮▮▮▮▮, ▮▮▮▮▮▮ and ▮▮▮▮▮▮, were noted for their ▮▮▮▮▮▮. In the king's court they were given Babylonian names: Daniel became ▮▮▮▮▮▮, a similar name to a later king. Daniel's three friends were renamed ▮▮▮▮▮▮ ▮▮▮▮▮▮ and ▮▮▮▮▮▮.

Their training was to continue three years under the king's chief, ▮▮▮▮▮▮. They were expected to learn ▮▮▮▮▮▮. Their food was the finest the king had to offer, but became the first arena of testing. Daniel had purposed in his heart ▮▮▮▮▮▮. He asked for a diet of ▮▮▮▮▮▮ and ▮▮▮▮▮▮. At first Ashpenaz was hesitant, but finally agreed to a ▮▮▮▮▮▮ trial, the end of which showed Daniel and his friends to be ▮▮▮▮▮▮ than others in training.

It was obvious to all that God had given these young men ▮▮▮▮▮▮. It was also obvious that ▮▮▮▮▮▮ had given Daniel the gift of ▮▮▮▮▮▮. One night king ▮▮▮▮▮▮ had a most perplexing dream, but could not remember ▮▮▮▮▮▮. He demanded that his ▮▮▮▮▮▮ tell the dream and interpret it. Their failure led to their anticipated ▮▮▮▮▮▮; that is, until Daniel respectfully approached ▮▮▮▮▮▮. He asked for ▮▮▮▮▮▮ from the king and for ▮▮▮▮▮▮ from his friends.

During the night, ▮▮▮▮▮▮ revealed the dream to Daniel. Rather than taking credit for himself, Daniel ▮▮▮▮▮▮. The dream contained a great ▮▮▮▮▮▮ made from ▮▮▮▮▮▮. It was a picture of the future kingdoms following ▮▮▮▮▮▮. It also became an object of pride as Nebuchadnezzar

INQUIRY–ACTION 31.1 (CONTINUED)

erected ⬜⬜⬜⬜⬜⬜⬜⬜⬜⬜⬜⬜ . At the sound of the ⬜⬜⬜⬜

⬜⬜⬜⬜⬜⬜ , all people had to ⬜⬜⬜⬜⬜⬜⬜⬜⬜ the image.

As Jews, Daniel's three friends, ⬜⬜⬜⬜⬜⬜⬜⬜⬜⬜⬜⬜⬜ ,
refused to worship any idol or ⬜⬜⬜⬜⬜⬜ . Thus, the king's fury was fueled;
so was the ⬜⬜⬜⬜⬜⬜ , seven times hotter than it had ever been before. The
friends confidently expressed their faith, "If you throw us into the furnace,
⬜⬜⬜⬜⬜⬜⬜⬜⬜⬜⬜⬜⬜⬜⬜ ." Looking into the fire,
Nebuchadnezzar was amazed to see ⬜⬜⬜⬜⬜⬜⬜⬜⬜⬜⬜
⬜⬜⬜⬜⬜⬜⬜⬜⬜⬜⬜⬜⬜ .

After coming forth from the fire, the three friends did not even have ⬜⬜⬜
⬜⬜⬜⬜⬜⬜⬜⬜ on their clothes. In praise, Nebuchadnezzar spoke of
⬜⬜⬜⬜⬜⬜⬜⬜⬜⬜⬜⬜⬜⬜⬜⬜ ,
and commanded that ⬜⬜⬜⬜⬜⬜⬜⬜⬜⬜ .

The second dream of Nebuchadnezzar's which Daniel interpreted was about
⬜⬜⬜⬜⬜⬜⬜⬜⬜⬜ . No doubt, Daniel feared telling the king that it
meant ⬜⬜⬜⬜⬜⬜⬜⬜⬜⬜⬜⬜⬜⬜⬜
⬜⬜⬜⬜⬜⬜⬜⬜⬜⬜ . That was the bad news. The good news was
⬜⬜⬜⬜⬜⬜⬜⬜⬜⬜⬜⬜⬜ . The dream came true
⬜⬜⬜⬜⬜⬜ later when the king became insane. For several years, he
⬜⬜⬜⬜⬜⬜⬜⬜⬜⬜⬜⬜⬜⬜⬜⬜ . Only when
Nebuchadnezzar recognized God was his ⬜⬜⬜⬜⬜⬜ restored.

Belshazzar was the next ⬜⬜⬜⬜⬜⬜ to come to power. One night he gave a
drunken party using ⬜⬜⬜⬜⬜⬜ from the Temple in Jerusalem. Suddenly, a
⬜⬜⬜⬜⬜⬜ appeared writing on the palace wall: Mene, Mene, Tekel,
Upharsin. The queen suggested that he ⬜⬜⬜⬜⬜⬜⬜⬜⬜⬜
⬜⬜⬜⬜ . Boldly Daniel challenged the king, "You have refused to be humble;
you have ⬜⬜⬜⬜⬜⬜⬜⬜⬜⬜⬜⬜⬜⬜
⬜⬜⬜⬜⬜⬜⬜⬜⬜⬜⬜⬜⬜⬜⬜⬜ ."

INQUIRY-ACTION 31.1 (CONTINUED)

This is what the words mean: Mene, _____ ,
Tekel, _____ , Peres,
_____ ."

That very night Belshazzar was _____ as the Babylonian kingdom
was conquered by the Medes and Persians.

Darius was the _____ under whom Daniel served.
Because of his _____ , Darius wanted to make him
ruler over all the kingdom. This so angered _____ that
they began to search for a way to _____ Daniel. Noting that Daniel
prayed _____ , they
devised a plot. In asking the king to decree that people were to pray to _____
_____ for _____ days, they feigned _____ to the
king and laid a trap for _____ .

When the king heard of Daniel's disobedience, he was _____ but the
law could not be repealed. Daniel was thrown to _____ . The next
_____ Darius hurried to the den to find Daniel unhurt and
_____ . "My God sent _____ to _____
the mouths of the lions." In retaliation, the king ordered that the administrators
be _____ .
Before they reached _____ of the den they were _____
_____ . Darius then wrote
_____ that superseded the previous one: Every person in my kingdom
must _____
because He is _____ . He has _____ Daniel from
_____ .

INQUIRY-ACTION 31.2

GOOD ADVICE FROM THE LIFE OF DANIEL

INQUIRY-ACTION 31.3

ROMANS 12:17–18

Restore the spaces and unscramble the letters in order to write the verses.

pearyononeveilorfivelahveeragrdorfoodggthisnin

ethighstfoallenmiftisipilessobachumsaddeepsn

onoyulevilayebpeachitwallenm

For fun, see how many words and names you can find in the letters as listed, and write them below.

MARY AND MARTHA

Surviving a Critical Spirit

In his 8th grade Bible class, Mr. Mitchell was always curious to know what the students were thinking. Frequently, he would distribute a brief survey for the students to complete. Sometimes the answers were pretty predictable. On other occasions he was surprised by the responses he received.

One day he surveyed his students using one simple question: "What things are junior high students most critical about?" After collecting the surveys, he tabulated the students' responses. Here's what he learned.

Junior high students were most critical about . . .

- the appearance of others or the clothes that they wore.
- the way other students talked or acted.
- teachers and homework.

Mr. Mitchell was not really surprised by these responses. Most students, no matter what their age, would have probably answered the same way. However, there were some responses on the surveys that he didn't expect. Think about why each of the following statements, reported on the student surveys, is so significant.

Students reported that junior highers are critical of . . .

- their parents, causing them to become isolated from the people who will prove over time to be their greatest supporters in the world.
- people who act like they are better than someone else.
- their friends who go to a Christian school and then don't act like a Christian should.

Do you see the difference between the first set of responses and the second three responses? Although having a critical spirit is never right, the first set focuses on preferences (appearance/clothes, teachers/homework). The second set of responses focuses on relationships with others (parents, friends, God).

From this survey a very important conclusion can be drawn: A critical spirit can become more serious if it is left unchecked. Typically, a critical spirit begins with dissatisfaction related to little things, like a gift received on a special occasion or a particular food item at mealtime. But as a critical spirit takes root, its bitter effects become more widespread. Soon, the individual gains the reputation as being negative and mean-spirited.

Our challenge this week is twofold. First, we must learn to curb our natural tendencies to be critical of others. Second, we need to learn how to better respond when others are critical of us. Both of these lessons are illustrated in the lives of Mary and Martha, friends of Jesus, who are mentioned in three events in Scripture.

When Jesus was upon this earth, He enjoyed going to the home of Mary, Martha and their brother Lazarus. According to Luke 10, after a time of exhausting teaching, Jesus went to their house for food and rest. While He talked, Mary sat at His feet; Martha continued to prepare the meal. Feeling pressured, Martha complained, "Lord, do you not care that my sister has left me to serve alone? Therefore tell her to help me" (Luke 10:40). What Martha felt inside was now expressed openly as criticism of Mary.

Jesus immediately stopped His teaching and turned His attention to Martha. Because of His love for these two sisters, Jesus was not willing to allow this critical spirit to continue. Jesus replied, "Martha, Martha, you are worried and troubled about many things. But one thing is needed, and Mary has chosen that good part, which will not be taken away from her" (Luke 10:41–42).

When Jesus said "Mary has chosen that good part," He reminded Martha that spiritual food was far more important than physical food. Mary was not avoiding serving the food. Her hunger for spiritual food caused her to forget about her physical hunger. Martha should not have criticized Mary for wanting to learn spiritual truth. Jesus made it very clear that Martha's criticism of her sister was wrong.

"Jesus wept" (John 11:35) is the shortest verse in the Bible. Its occasion was the death of Lazarus and the sorrow of his two sisters, Mary and Martha. Jesus had risked his life to come to Bethany in response to the sisters' request. Prior to calling Lazarus from the tomb, Jesus spoke some of the most encouraging words of the Bible: "I am the resurrection and the life. He who believes in Me, though he may die, he shall live" (John 11:25).

During the weekend prior to the Crucifixion, we again encounter these friends of Jesus—this time at a large banquet at the home of Simon, perhaps Martha's deceased husband. During the evening, Mary used a bottle of expensive perfume to anoint Jesus' head then feet in preparation for his death. Judas hotly criticized her actions, stating that the money could have been better used to feed the poor. Jesus spoke in Mary's defense, "Let her alone. Why do you trouble her? She has done a good work for me . . . wherever this gospel is preached in the whole world, what this woman has done will also be told as a memorial to her" (Mark 14:6, 9).

Every day, in many different ways, you will hear people criticize others. Does the constant criticism of others bother you? Do you enjoy being around people who put others down? Have you ever felt that the critical spirit of others has rubbed off on you?

There are two facts about a critical spirit that are undeniable.

- No one likes to be around a person with a critical spirit.
- Those who have a critical spirit are not happy people.

Proverbs 12:18 compares a critical spirit to the "piercings of a sword." Criticism seriously wounds others. Just as the repeated piercing of a sword would physically kill a person, the repeated piercing of criticism destroys the spirit and joy of others. In God's sight, there are no good reasons to be critical of others. The answer to a critical spirit is the "joy of the Lord" in your life. A life of celebration has no time for a critical spirit. It is impossible to be critical and joyful at the same time.

The strategy for learning how to survive a critical spirit is learning how to celebrate life. In other words, joy—not criticism—becomes the pattern of our thinking and speaking. This transformation in our lives can take place when the following steps are taken.

Step 1: Make a daily choice for joy.

You have a lot more control over your attitude than you might think. When you get up in the morning, you can choose to be difficult to get along with, to worry about what is going to happen that day and to be critical of the things and people around you. Start tomorrow differently! When you get up, focus on the blessings and opportunities that God has set before you. Determine that your words throughout the day will be positive rather than judgmental. It's a choice that only you can make.

Step 2: Choose at least one friend who will encourage your pursuit of joy.

This may be the hardest step for you to take. Typically, critical people associate with other critical people. If you want to overcome a critical spirit, you must avoid those who are critical and seek to be around those who are positive and joyful. Just as a critical spirit rubs off on others, so will a joyful spirit.

Step 3: Celebrate God's goodness in your life.

It is so easy to be caught up in complaining that we fail to see the blessings that God bestows upon us each day. Suppose you knew, for a fact, that your life would come to an end 24 hours from right now. Who would you miss, what opportunity would you lose or what things would you have to leave behind? Sometimes we are so focused on criticizing and complaining that we are unaware of the incredible blessings and gifts that God has given to us. Set aside a regular time to thank God for what He is doing in your life. Ask Him to recreate His spirit in you—a spirit that seeks life's harmony, not destruction and death.

Step 4: Test every word and action.

"Think before you speak" is good advice. Your words can be used for great good or great evil. How will you test them? Simply ask: Do they promote life or death?

Can you remember the last time that you criticized someone? Do you remember what you said? Did you say things that weren't quite true about that person? Was your attitude mean? Did you try to get others to also criticize that person? Suppose that right in the middle of your criticism of the person, you looked over your shoulder and saw Jesus standing there. Would that have changed what you said? Would your attitude be different?

When Martha criticized Mary, her sister, Jesus was right there. When Judas criticized Mary, Jesus heard what he said and how he said it. It's no different today. Jesus continues to hear all of your conversations. Is He pleased with what He hears?

INQUIRY-ACTION 32.1

CRITICISM BUGS

Adults	Other Students
1. _____	1. _____
2. _____	2. _____
3. _____	3. _____
4. _____	4. _____
5. _____	5. _____

My Critical Spirit That Bugs Them

_____   _____
_____   _____
_____   _____
_____   _____

INQUIRY-ACTION 32.2

WHAT'S MORE IMPORTANT TO YOU?

_____	> time
_____	> body
_____	> sacrifice
_____	> things
_____	> actions
_____	> talk
_____	> being served
_____	> wealth
_____	> talent
_____	> man's approval

In view of what's really important, how then will you live?

_____

_____

_____

_____

_____

INQUIRY-ACTION 32.3

_____
Date

Dear Lord,

    In learning about the importance of priori-
ties, I am promising myself to _____

_____

_____

_____

_____

    I humbly ask your help in living out this

promise.

                         Sincerely,

                        _____

INQUIRY-ACTION 32.4

PSALM 100

Fill in the blanks to write the verses.

M_ _ _ _ _ _ y_ _ _ _ _ _ _ t

_ _ _ h_ _ _ r_ ,

_ _ l _ _ _ _ _ _ d _ !

_ _ _ _ v_ _ _ e _ o_ _

_ _ t_ _ _ _ d _ _ _ _ ;

_ _ m_ _ _ f_ _ _ _ _ s

_ _ _ s_ _ _ _ _ _ t_

_ _ _ g_ _ _ .

_ n_ _ _ _ _ t t_ _ _ _ _ d ,

_ e i_ _ o_ ;

_ t _ _ _ e _ h_ _ _ _ _ _ d _

_ s , _ n_ n_ _ _ _ _

_ _ _ s_ _ _ _ .

INQUIRY-ACTION 32.4 (CONTINUED)

_ e _ _ e _ i _ _ _ o _ _ _

 a _ t _ _ _ h _ _ _ _ f

_ i _ _ _ _ t _ _ _ .

_ n _ _ _ _ n _ _ _ i _ _ _ t _ _

_ i _ _ _ _ _ _ k _ _ _ _ _ _ _ ,

_ n _ n _ _ i _ _ _ _ _ t _

_ i _ _ _ _ _ _ s _ .

_ e _ _ _ _ _ f _ _ _ o _ i _ ,

_ _ d _ _ _ s _ _ i _ _ m _ .

_ o _ t _ _ _ o _ _ _ _ _ o _ ;

_ _ s _ _ _ c _ _ _ _ _

_ _ _ _ _ l _ _ _ _ _ _ _ ,

_ n _ _ i _ r _ _ _ _ _ _

_ _ d _ _ _ _ t _ _ l _ _

_ _ _ _ _ r _ _ _ _ _ .

SAMUEL

Surviving Obstacles to Success

The story is told of a man who had been on a hiking expedition with a number of his friends. One day he was separated from the group and became lost in the dense woods. For days he wandered around aimlessly. Although he was able to find nuts and berries to eat, he had no water. His thirst eventually became unbearable.

Late one afternoon he came upon an old shack that had probably been abandoned for at least ten years. As he looked around, he stumbled upon an old, rusty water pump. He quickly grabbed the handle and began to pump as fast as he could. The pump was dry; not a single drop of water emerged from the spout. The old pump would not work without pouring water into the spout—a process called priming.

Suddenly, he noticed an old jug just a few feet away from the water pump. He picked it up, wiped away the dirt and read the following message, "The pump will not work unless you prime it. Use all of the water in this jug."

He unscrewed the cap and was amazed to find that the jug was full of water. Suddenly, he was faced with a difficult decision. Should he just drink the water in the jug? There was enough water to last at least a couple of days. Or should he take a chance and use the water to prime the old, rusty water pump? If the pump failed, all of the water would be wasted.

He thought about it for a long time. Reluctantly, he lifted the jug and poured all of the water into the pump. Immediately, he started pumping the handle as rapidly as he could. No water came out. He frantically kept pumping. Nothing! He was approaching the point of panic when all of a sudden, a blend of dust mixed with water spurted out of the pump. The sight of success caused him to pump harder.

A small stream of water emerged. Within moments, fresh, clear water gushed from the pump.

The man filled the jug and drank the cool, fresh water. He filled the jug again and poured the water over his face and head. He then filled the jug a third time and placed the cap tightly back in place. As someone had once left a jug of water for his use, he would leave a full jug of water for the next traveler.

The message to use the water to prime the pump was still on the jug. The man decided to add the following words of encouragement to the note: "Don't let your thirst get in the way of following the instructions. Use all the water in the jug, and you'll have more water than you need!"

The man's thirst had almost caused him to drink the water rather than use it to prime the pump. Fortunately, he did not allow the obstacle—his thirst—to get in the way of making the right decision. Unfortunately, there are many people who don't overcome the obstacles they face. As a result, they never achieve the happiness and success that God has intended for them.

The prophet Samuel knew what it was like to face obstacles. For years, during the time of the judges, Israel strayed farther and farther away from God. After Samson's death, the nation was without leadership, both spiritually and militarily. God raised up Samuel to lead Israel as well as restore religious life in the nation. But Samuel faced many serious obstacles.

The first obstacle concerned Israel's military problems. The Philistines, who had oppressed Israel during the time of Samson, were still in the land. The people were afraid to tend their flocks or work in the fields because of the constant Philistine attacks.

The second obstacle Samuel faced was the terrible sin of the people. For over 400 years, the people had continued to worship false gods and marry those from the surrounding nations. After all of these years, the worship of the God of Israel was no longer important. The sacrifices and ceremonies had been forgotten. The religion of the Israelites had become a "mixture" of the religions of all the surrounding nations.

The religious leadership was the third obstacle that Samuel faced. The priests and Levites had initially been established by God to explain the Law, conduct the ceremonies and teach the people God's way. Instead, they had corrupted the places of worship by using their positions for personal gain. They made money through buying and selling animals at the places of sacrifice. The religious leaders had become more concerned with profit than the spiritual condition of the people.

Samuel next faced the obstacle of rejection. Because other nations had kings, Israel clamored for a king. Rather than trusting God for leadership, they insisted on a human leader. Knowing that the people had rejected Him, God chose Saul to fill this role.

The final obstacle Samuel faced was the disobedience of Saul. In the first event, Saul presumptuously refused to wait for Samuel to offer sacrifices. Ignoring the warning, Saul foolishly disobeyed God during a second event. Samuel became God's voice to declare that the kingdom would be torn from Saul and given to another.

The right attitude: God is greater than the obstacles.

If success is 10% dependent on aptitude and 90% dependent on attitude, then Samuel's life teaches us some important lessons. Faced with similar obstacles, most people would have given up. But Samuel knew that the God he served was greater than the obstacles. If God had a task for Samuel to do, He would not let the obstacles stand in his way.

When was the last time an obstacle stood in your way of doing what God wanted you to do? Maybe there is someone in your class who is being made fun of by others. Of course, this does not honor the Lord. You know you should speak up and defend that person but are afraid of what others will think of you. This fear is an obstacle in your life to doing what is right. Turn the obstacle into an opportunity to strengthen your walk with the Lord.

Control the fear that restricts your action.

Samuel was also able to overcome the obstacles because he continued in the pathway that God had prepared for him. So often, people try to be someone they're not.

This could have easily happened to Samuel. Until the time of Samuel, Israel had been led by military leaders. It would have been easy for him to think that God wanted him to be a military leader.

Follow your own drum beat.

But God had not prepared Samuel for battle. God had prepared him for spiritual warfare. The sin of the people and the corruption of the religious leaders were the obstacles Samuel had to face. His years of preparation were for this task. He was to be a religious leader, not a military leader. When you face obstacles in your life, don't try to be someone different from how God has prepared you.

Finally, Samuel was able to overcome the obstacles because he used the good sense (wisdom) that God had given to him. Repeatedly, we are told that Samuel heard the voice of God. All too often we make decisions based upon our emotions and not upon common sense.

Develop common-sense wisdom.

When faced with a challenge in your life, don't respond immediately. A quick decision is often based upon emotions at the moment rather than good information and logical thinking. Samuel overcame the obstacles he faced after careful deliberation. We must do the same.

Everyone faces obstacles in life. The test of your character is what you do when you face them. Always remember:

Obstacles are opportunities in disguise!

INQUIRY-ACTION 33.1

Summarize each area of Samuel's life.

Title:

Title:

Title:

INQUIRY-ACTION 33.1 (CONTINUED)

Title:

Title:

Title:

Title:

INQUIRY-ACTION 33.2
HOW TO HAVE SUCCESS WITH GOD

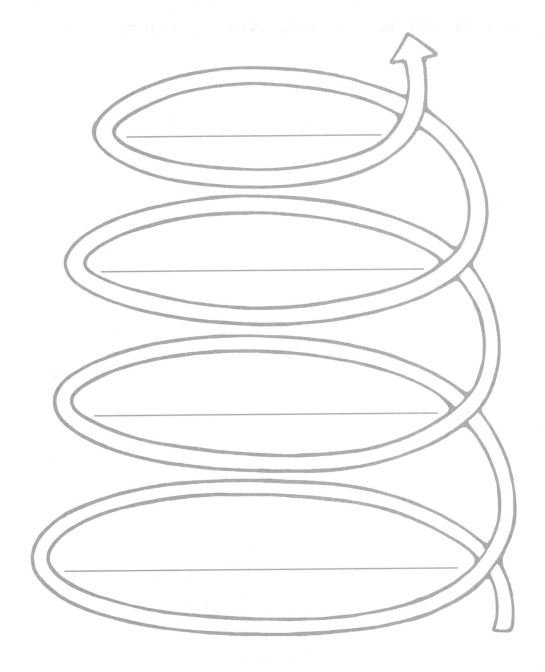

Inquiry–Action 33.3

1 Samuel 15:22

Place letters into the boxes to complete the words of the verse.

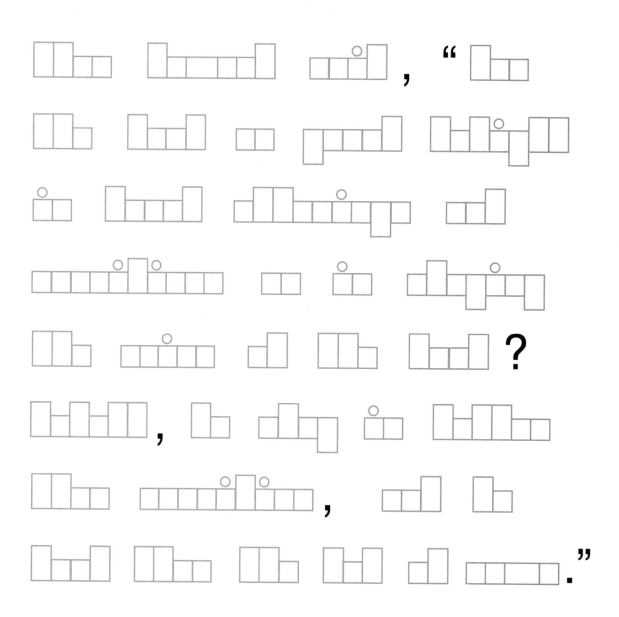

ELIJAH

Surviving Discouragement

Your brain is the most amazing organ in your body. The largest and most complex part of your nervous system, it is composed of billions of neurons and innumerable nerve synapses. Every part of your body is connected, in one way or another, to your brain.

Stop for a moment and think about some of the amazing things that go on in your brain. In the brain . . .

- the coordination of every muscle in your body is directed.
- the light that enters your eyes is interpreted into meaningful images.
- various bits of information are combined to enable you to solve a problem.
- your memory holds onto images and sounds, sometimes for years, until they are needed.
- is the control center for the regulation of your body's growth.

As a result of these and other incredible activities in your brain, thousands of thoughts are generated every day. That is why the Apostle Peter said, " . . . gird up . . . your mind" (1 Peter 1:13). It is your mind that controls your emotions, speech and actions. If your thoughts are not properly regulated, you will lose control of your life.

Deep inside your brain is the amygdala, which controls your emotional responses. Depending on the degree of threat it perceives, your emotions can completely swamp the more logical thought centers of your brain. This response releases various chemicals throughout your body to prepare you to face danger. This instantaneous response can save your life. Stress can create the same biochemical response. Over time, this chemical imbalance can produce discouragement and depression.

Pretend that there are two foremen controlling your thoughts. One is called Mr. Discouragement, and the other goes by the name of Mr. Victorious. Every time something happens in your life, both men are there to interpret the event for you.

Suppose you took a test and missed more questions than you thought you should. Mr. Discouragement is right there to suggest that you are stupid, the test was not fair, the teacher doesn't like you or that the class is a waste of time. On the other hand, Mr. Victorious encourages you to evaluate the situation differently. He reminds you that you won't make the same mistake next time or that this is just a bump in the road to success.

Doesn't it seem as if a Mr. Discouragement and Mr. Victorious are present in your mind? It might be said that both were present in Elijah's life. First Kings records two stories, one in Chapter 18 and the other in Chapter 19, which show Elijah's two very different responses. In the first story, Mr. Victorious was in charge. However, in Chapter 19 Mr. Discouragement was in complete control of Elijah's thoughts and actions.

Elijah was a man with a mission. As a prophet, he was authorized by God to speak for Him. One of the responsibilities of a prophet was to reveal sin and call for repentance. This became Elijah's job in the lives of King Ahab and Queen Jezebel.

Ahab and Jezebel were from different backgrounds. King Ahab was an Israelite and Queen Jezebel was a Phoenician from the city of Tyre. As an Israelite, Ahab was to worship Jehovah. Jezebel worshiped a pagan god named Baal. As a result of their marriage, Ahab agreed to make Jezebel's god equal to the God of Israel. Numerous idols honoring Baal were established to plead for fertility. This greatly displeased the Lord. As a result, Elijah was sent to confront Ahab and Jezebel with their sin.

According to 1 Kings 17:1, there would be no rain in the land of Israel. It was three years before God allowed the rain to return. In the meantime, Israel experienced great drought and famine. The three-year drought was God's way of getting Ahab and Jezebel's attention and proving the futility of worshiping idols.

When Elijah returned at the end of three years, Ahab and Jezebel furiously blamed him for all the trouble experienced in Israel. However, Elijah was unafraid. If there was ever a time that a Mr. Victorious was in control of Elijah's mind, it was now. Elijah had seen God withhold the rain for three years. He not only knew that God was in control, he knew that God had sent him to this wicked king and queen with the message of repentance.

But God was not finished. It was now time for Him to really send the message that He was the True God. The showdown between Elijah's God and Ahab and Jezebel's god took place on Mount Carmel. According to 1 Kings 18:20-40, the victory that Elijah experienced was one of the greatest triumphs recorded in the Bible. Can you imagine what Elijah was thinking as he watched the destruction of the false prophets and the humiliation of their god? Through this victory, Elijah experienced great boldness and confidence.

But in the next chapter (1 Kings 19), Mr. Victorious was no longer present in Elijah's life. Mr. Discouragement had now taken over. It all began in verse two when Jezebel sent a messenger to Elijah informing him that he would be dead by the next day.

Elijah, who had just watched God miraculously destroy the false prophets and their god, was unable to trust God to protect him from Jezebel. When you read 1 Kings 19:3–18, you can tell that Mr. Discouragement was in control. Note that Elijah . . .

- was scared to death.
- ran away.
- abandoned his servant so that no one would know where he went.
- requested that he might die.
- was physically exhausted.
- felt he was a total failure.
- was sure he was the only believer left.
- was disappointed and angry with God.

The prophet who had just experienced a great victory at Mount Carmel was now running for his life and wanted to die. That is how quickly discouragement can take control in our lives. We can fall from the mountain of success into the pit of despair, seemingly without warning. Once Mr. Discouragement is in control, we lose our joy and our ability to think clearly.

Notice that God did not scold Elijah for the way he responded. He knew that Elijah was discouraged. So God took steps to encourage him. He provided Elijah with food to strengthen him. He sent an angel to comfort him. God told Elijah that He would take care of his enemies for him. God gave him his assignment for continuing service. Finally, God reminded Elijah that he was not alone. There were 7000 more like him who were faithful and had not bowed to Jezebel and her false gods.

God knew that in order for Elijah to overcome discouragement, he needed a new perspective. Elijah's earthly perspective was that he was alone, without hope, and would soon die. God gave Elijah an eternal perspective. It was this heavenly perspective that enabled Elijah to overcome his discouragement.

Everyone experiences times of discouragement. That's why God recorded Elijah's story. If you don't believe that, read Romans 15:4, "For whatever things were written before were written for our learning, that we through the patience and comfort of the Scriptures might have hope." But don't stop reading there. Read the next two verses, "Now may the God of patience and comfort grant you to be likeminded toward one another, according to Christ Jesus, that you may with one mind and one mouth glorify the God and Father of our Lord Jesus Christ."

Notice that these last two verses focus on the mind. It is the mind that directs all that we think, say and do. That's why it is so important to pattern our thinking after the Lord Jesus Christ. When we have an eternal perspective, Mr. Discouragement can never be in control. When we have His mind, we have an eternal perspective.

INQUIRY-ACTION 34.1

NEWSCAST FORMAT

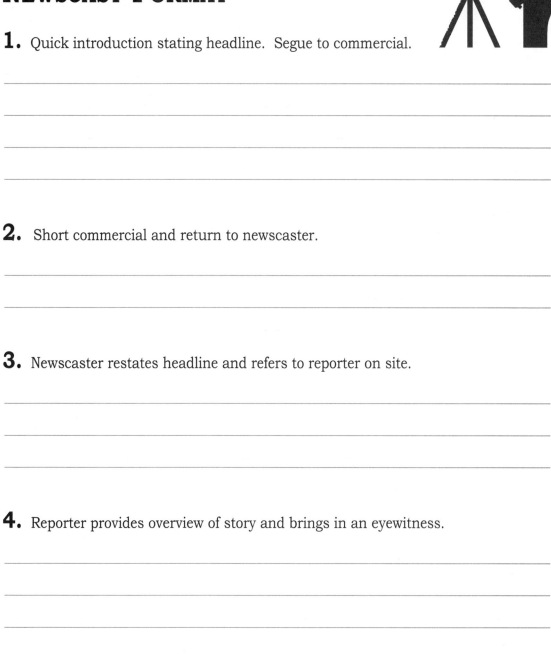

1. Quick introduction stating headline. Segue to commercial.

_____

_____

_____

_____

2. Short commercial and return to newscaster.

_____

_____

3. Newscaster restates headline and refers to reporter on site.

_____

_____

_____

4. Reporter provides overview of story and brings in an eyewitness.

_____

_____

_____

_____

Inquiry-Action 34.1 (CONTINUED)

5. Eyewitness gives personal description of events.

_____

_____

_____

_____

6. Reporter summarizes and states several unanswered questions or continuing controversies.

_____

_____

_____

7. Newscaster quickly states overview of story and segues to another commercial.

_____

_____

_____

8. Short commercial.

_____

_____

INQUIRY-ACTION 34.2

DISPELLING DISCOURAGEMENT

Write on the clouds things that cause discouragement.
Write on the puddles symptoms of discouragement.
Write on the sunbeams ways to overcome discouragement.

INQUIRY-ACTION 34.3

ROMANS 15:5–6

Begin at the circled N and move from block to block to locate all the words in the verses.

G	R	I	S	O	T	Y	D	O	R	A	D
C	H	A	W	A	R	E	N	I	L	O	R
H	C	E	N	O	D	U	M	E	K	I	L
R	W	A	N	E	M	A	Y	O	Y	E	B
D	N	O	N	O	W	I	T	A	T	O	T
H	T	E	F	O	D	O	H	I	N	U	R
T	H	O	P	A	G	E	D	O	M	A	G
G	T	E	T	E	N	I	C	A	F	Y	T
L	C	A	R	I	C	E	D	U	S	O	R
S	C	O	R	O	N	A	N	E	J	U	S
W	N	E	D	I	G	O	C	Y	T	A	T
N	M	O	T	I	T	I	H	I	S	A	H
C	N	I	H	O	W	Y	R	O	T	O	T
R	D	A	N	E	Y	A	M	U	Y	U	S
D	N	O	D	O	F	O	F	E	R	I	C
N	M	E	M	U	H	T	Y	U	R	O	R
G	L	O	R	I	G	O	R	O	L	I	H
H	T	U	H	Y	F	A	T	O	F	A	C
L	G	E	T	U	D	E	H	E	R	U	S
R	D	O	D	A	N	E	T	Y	D	E	S
D	M	I	N	O	S	U	S	E	J	Y	T

LUKE

Surviving Challenges of Service

For a moment, let's take a look at two unusual families serving the Lord on opposite sides of the world. What makes them so unusual is that neither of the families are missionaries in the way that we normally think of missionaries. Both of the husband and wife teams have unique skills. However, instead of using their skills to provide a comfortable living for themselves in the United States, they are using their skills to serve others.

To reach Jim and Donna's base of service, you would have to prepare yourself for a very long trip. Your "jumping-off" point would be Miami, Florida. From there you would take a five-hour flight to Belem. If you look on a map of South America, you see it located on the coast of Brazil where the Para River empties into the Atlantic Ocean.

After you change planes, you are ready for your flight to Manaus, 1500 miles to the west deep in the heart of Brazil. It is the city where the Rio Negro River and Amazon River come together to form the Amazon. It is the only outpost of civilization for hundreds of miles.

In Manaus you must board a shallow riverboat for the 80-mile trip down the Amazon. It might be a good idea if you keep your hands out of the water. The Amazon River is filled with flesh-eating piranha.

Finally, you will see Jim and Donna's outpost carved from the jungle on the eastern bank. You are likely to be surprised by a lot of things you see. The first is a twenty-foot climb up the river's bank. The buildings along the cliff are not houses; most of them look like dormitories. The entire area is no more than 150 yards wide and about 50 yards deep. Even then it takes constant effort to prevent the jungle from overtaking the land.

Probably the most surprising thing you will see is that Jim and Donna are sur-rounded by children. Lots of them! Their base of service is a small boarding school for missionary children. The parents of these children are reaching the tribes living deep in the jungle. While the parents are spreading the Gospel, their children live and attend school at the base camp.

Jim and Donna are not teachers. They are professional psychologists capable of earning six-figure salaries. Here they serve as the "dorm parents" for these MKs. Rather than developing a private practice, they have dedicated their talents to serv-ing the children of missionaries.

Our second missionary couple is Randy and Ann, who serve the Lord in a very dif-ferent part of the world—St. Petersburg, Russia. St. Petersburg is approximately 600 miles north of Moscow at about the same parallel as Anchorage, Alaska. Some of the most beautiful architecture in the world is found in this city. St. Petersburg was the summer home to the Czars, the rulers of Russia prior to the Communist revolution.

Before coming to St. Petersburg, Randy and Ann were intelligence officers in the Army—Russian intelligence. They actually met while they were in the Army serving as language translators. Though both of them were born in the United States, they speak Russian with native fluency.

During their tours of duty in the Army, they accepted the Lord as their Savior. After leaving the Army, they were determined to find a place that they could serve the Lord. The only logical place was Russia. They knew the language and they loved the people. They were confident that the Lord had provided the opportunity to learn Russian so that they could use their skills in His service. Today, Randy and Ann faithfully serve the Lord as translators for Christian organizations throughout Russia.

Unfortunately, many Christians believe that the only way that you can serve the Lord is if you preach or teach. But the opportunity to serve the Lord exists in every vocation. Just as there are couples like Jim and Donna and Randy and Ann using their skills for the Lord today, the same was true centuries ago. Luke also used his training to serve the Lord during the formation of the early church.

Luke was trained as a physician. Most everyone knows that he wrote the gospel of Luke. But there are many who do not realize that he also wrote the book of Acts. Luke wrote both of these books because he was an eyewitness to the two most important events that took place during the First Century: Jesus' ministry and Paul's missionary journeys. In his gospel, Luke describes the birth, ministry and crucifixion of Jesus. Because of his professional training, he provides a very detailed account of Jesus' physical life.

In the book of Acts, Luke explains how the early church was formed and what took place on Paul's three missionary journeys. Luke was able to tell the story because he was there. He traveled with Paul on all of his journeys. He served Paul as both a traveling companion and with his medical skills.

It is 2 Timothy 4:11 that gives us insight as to the extent of Luke's faithful service. Second Timothy was written by Paul from a Roman prison. As he wrote his last words shortly before his death, Paul noted, "Only Luke is with me." Luke served Paul right to the end. Although everyone else deserted Paul, Luke remained faithful to him.

There is no question that Luke faced a number of challenges as he served the Lord. That faithful service was a deliberate choice. Like Simon Peter in Luke 5:1–11, Luke made a personal commitment to follow the Lord. Throughout his years of service, in spite of the challenges he survived, he knew that there was no turning back. He determined to follow the Lord.

Serving the Lord means choosing to follow . . .

. . . even when you don't understand where you are going. When the twelve disciples chose to follow the Lord, they had no idea where they would be going and what they would be doing. If you're like most people, you want to know what's going to happen each day. But if you choose to serve the Lord, you need to be willing to follow Him even if you don't know what lies ahead. If you can trust His leadership in your life, you will be able to survive the challenges of service.

. . . even when you don't feel like it. In Luke 9:23 the Lord reminded His disciples that if they were going to follow Him, they would have to "deny" themselves. That means that they would have to put their service and devotion to the Lord above their own personal desires. God does not seek "Sunshine Servants" who are only willing to serve Him when it's convenient or they feel like it. He wants those who are willing to "deny" themselves the things of this world. If you can put serving the Lord above serving yourself, you will be able to survive the challenges of service.

. . . even though everyone is going a different way. The Christian is constantly reminded that he or she should not be conformed to the world (Romans 12:2). You know how strong the temptation is to give in to the worldly lifestyle that surrounds you every day. But conforming to Christ is what God calls us to do. If may be hard for you to believe, but you can still have fun and be liked by others while maintaining a godly testimony. If you can stand firm for your beliefs, in spite of what others think, you will be able to survive the challenges of service.

. . . even if it costs you everything. The Lord Jesus Christ was willing to give His life on the Cross for your sins. That is why He said in Luke 14:33 "So likewise, whoever of you who does not forsake all that he has cannot be my disciple." Serving the Lord means that you are willing to give up everything—even your life—to do His will. This is not an unrealistic expectation. Even at your age, young people have made this type of commitment to the Lord. If you are willing to lay down your life for the Lord, you will be able to survive the challenges of service.

Are you willing to follow?
Are you willing to serve?
Are you willing to accept the challenges?

INQUIRY-ACTION 35.1

THE APOSTLE LUKE

Writer of:

_____

and

_____

Why he is not well known:

_____

_____

Best known for:

_____

and

_____

His vocations:

_____

and

_____

Unique features
of his writings:

_____

_____

_____

Most unusual
facts learned:

_____

_____

_____

INQUIRY-ACTION 35.2

So What's Important?
Studies in Luke

Topic	Application to Life
Salvation 2:30–31 19:9–10 13:3 15:6–7 24:46–47	
Following the Lord 12:8–9 14:33 17:33 18:29–30	
Faithfulness 9:62 12:41–44 12:47–48 16:10–12	
Servant Attitude 6:31–36 17:9–10 18:13–14 22:24–27	

INQUIRY-ACTION 35.2 (CONTINUED)

Treatment of Children

2:40

9:48

18:15–17

_____

_____

_____

Treatment of Poor and Disabled

4:18–19

7:22

14:12–14

14:22–23

_____

_____

_____

_____

Prayer

11:9–13

22:45–46

_____

_____

Investing in Eternal Treasure

6:38, 45

9:25

12:22–24

12:29–31

16:13–15

_____

_____

_____

_____

_____

INQUIRY-ACTION 35.3

1 CORINTHIANS 4:1-2

The numerals indicate the number of letters in the words that form the verse. Decipher the verse and write it below.

3	1	3	2	8	2,
2	8	2	6	3	8
2	3	9	2	3.	
8	2	2	8	2	8
4	3	2	5	8.	

_____

_____

_____

_____

_____

_____

_____

Application to Life: _____

_____

_____

_____

REVIEW

Let me introduce you to the "Eggshell" family. Mr. and Mrs. Eggshell do not take risks, never "rock the boat," do not know what it means to live by faith. Mr. and Mrs. Eggshell have become so afraid that they won't even pick up the telephone when it rings.

According to Mr. Eggshell, "If we pick it up, there might be somebody on the other end who wants to talk with me. What would I say? I could be asked a question. Then I would have to answer. Eventually, someone would have to hang up the telephone. Should I do it first? If I did hang up first, would I offend the other person?" With that, Mr. Eggshell buried his head in his hands. No matter what happened, he would never, never, never pick up a ringing telephone.

And then, of course, there is Mrs. Eggshell. Her story is just as frightening. One day the doorbell rang. She just knew that someone was on the other side of the door. Should she open it? If someone was there, she would have to speak to the person. What would she say? Perhaps the person had bad news. Then what?

"I continued to let the doorbell ring," she said. "I was afraid that there might be someone on the other side of the door that might want to talk with me. I couldn't take that chance. Finally, the doorbell quit ringing. I guess there wasn't anyone there after all."

Do you see any of the characteristics of the Eggshell family in your life? Are you afraid to step out of your comfort zone? Do you become nervous when you are faced with a new challenge? Is your life "on hold" because you don't want to take any risks?

SurvivalQuest has been about a journey. It is about your journey as you face the challenges of life and grow in your relationship with the Lord. In order to successfully complete your quest, you will have to step outside of your comfort zone. The journey of life is not always an easy one. There are many personal struggles that must be overcome. As you have seen throughout this Bible study, God provides the necessary direction as you face the obstacles on life's journey.

Take a moment and carefully review the following list of "survival challenges" you studied this semester:

Surviving Position and Possessions	**Esther**
Surviving Destructive Anger	**Cain and Abel**
Surviving Wrong Motives	**Jonah**
Surviving Life Changes	**Paul**
Surviving Habits of Deception	**Jacob**
Surviving Unrealistic Expectations	**Deborah**
Surviving Personal Inadequacies	**Moses**
Surviving Bad Things That Happen	**Job**
Surviving Loneliness	**John**
Surviving a Poor Background	**Othniel**
Surviving Ridicule and Vengeance	**Noah**
Surviving Unfulfilled Dreams	**Solomon**
Surviving False Accusations	**Daniel**
Surviving a Critical Spirit	**Mary and Martha**
Surviving Obstacles to Success	**Samuel**
Surviving Discouragement	**Elijah**
Surviving Challenges of Service	**Luke**

As you reviewed the list, did you realize that you are struggling with at least one of these challenges right now? If so, go back to that chapter and review the principles of "surviving and thriving" contained there. Unlike the Eggshell family, you don't need to fear that you will crack. Actually, an eggshell is very tough. So are you! With God's help, you can take risks, work on solutions and be an overcomer. You can survive and thrive!

Jesus said in John 16:33, "These things I have spoken to you, that in Me you may have peace. In the world you will have tribulation; but be of good cheer, I have overcome the world." The Christian life is a life of "overcoming" the world. Each of the lessons in *SurvivalQuest* has been prepared to help you overcome and survive the challenges in your life. It is now up to you to endure and finish strong!

The following steps will help you finish strong in your Christian walk.

Step 1: Prioritize what is most important in your life. How important is it to you that you obey the Lord in every aspect of your life? In Luke 16:13 Jesus reminds us that we cannot serve two masters. We cannot say that God is Number One and also say that we want to be like others in the world. The two are incompatible. The Lord reminds us that we must choose who will set the priorities in our life. In order to finish strong, your priorities must honor the Lord.

Step 2: Understand that God has uniquely created you for a reason. There is no one else in the whole world exactly like you. That's no accident. You are His creation, He knows you by name (Isaiah 43:1). When you face difficulties along life's journey, don't be afraid. God will not leave you. You have been created for a reason. In order to finish strong, you must always remember the special place that you hold in God's plan.

Step 3: Resolve that no matter where God places you in the years to come, you will do your best to serve Him. After you finish school, you will enter the world of work. Maybe you already know what kind of work you want to do for the rest of your life. Maybe you haven't given it very much thought. However, regardless of how you earn your living, you will always have the opportunity to serve the Lord. In order to finish strong, you must serve the Lord in whatever place you are (Colossians 3:24).

Step 4: Prayerfully express your commitment to the Lord and seek His strength in your life. Making a personal commitment to the Lord is a serious matter. It is not a decision made today and forgotten next week. The psalmist (Psalm 46) realized that God alone was his protection and strength. In order to finish strong, you must seek guidance and strength through prayer.

Step 5: Organize your priorities around God's priorities. Jesus said, "But seek first the kingdom of God and His righteousness . . ." (Matthew 6:33). God's number one priority for us is to seek Him and serve Him. Unfortunately, that is not the number one priority for most Christians. What are the three most important things in your life? Is seeking and serving God even in your top three? In order to finish strong, your priorities must be God's priorities.

Step 6: Endure difficulties by staying focused on your goal. Sometimes when problems arise, there is the temptation to turn away from the Lord. As you journey down your personal pathway of life, there are two important principles to remember:

- Principle One: You will experience difficulties in life.

- Principle Two: God will enable you to survive the difficulties.

Remember what Jesus said in John 16:33—that you can have peace even though you will have tribulation, and that you should be of good cheer because He has overcome the world. Both principles are outlined in this verse. In order to finish strong, you must stay focused on your goal—in spite of the difficulties!

Let's return to the home of Mr. and Mrs. Eggshell. If you could peek through the living room window, you would see both of them sitting comfortably on their favorite chairs. As long as the telephone doesn't ring or someone doesn't knock on the door, they're content. Their lives revolve totally around themselves. They avoid anything that will disrupt their own little world.

Don't be a Christian version of the Eggshell family. You cannot avoid the tribulations of life. You cannot pretend that you will never experience difficulties. God wants you to survive, not be defeated by, the topics studied this year. As you pursue your own *SurvivalQuest*, keep the following promises of God in mind:

- *Wait on the Lord; be of good courage, and He shall strengthen your heart. (Psalm 27:14)*

- *Fear thou not, for I am with you; be not dismayed, for I am your God. I will strengthen you, Yes, I will help you. I will uphold you with My righteous right hand. (Isaiah 41:10)*

- *Serve the Lord with gladness; come before His presence with singing. (Psalm 100:2)*

- *Trust in the Lord with all your heart, and lean not on your own understanding; in all your ways acknowledge Him, and He shall direct your paths. (Proverbs 3:5–6)*

Inquiry-Action 36.1

Review It or Lose It

Bible Character: _____

Summary of Life: _____

_____

_____

Challenge/s faced by the character:

_____

_____

Three important principles I have learned about surviving and thriving when facing this challenge:

   1) _____

   2) _____

   3) _____

The main reason students do not have success in facing this challenge:

_____

_____

Example of how I can survive and thrive in this challenge:

_____

_____

INQUIRY-ACTION 36.2

REVIEW IT OR LOSE IT

Bible Character: _____

Summary of Life: _____

_____

_____

Challenge/s faced by the character:

_____

_____

Three important principles I have learned about surviving and thriving when facing this challenge:

1) _____

2) _____

3) _____

The main reason students do not have success in facing this challenge:

_____

_____

Example of how I can survive and thrive in this challenge:

_____

_____

Inquiry-Action 36.3

Final Commitment

Your paper will not be seen by anyone except you. Your honesty will allow God to work as you develop godly character.

✔ The one truth from this course that has been most important to me is . . .

_____

✔ A challenge area which I feel confident in handling is . . .

_____

✔ The challenge area that needs most improvement in how I handle things is . . .

_____

✔ The biggest obstacle to my improving this area is . . .

_____

✔ Some things I want to work on are . . .

_____

_____

✔ I want to commit myself to developing godly character.   Yes ☐   No ☐
If yes, complete the next page.

INQUIRY-ACTION 36.4

Commitment to Successfully Facing the Challenges of Life

Based on the challenges presented in this course, I am willing to commit myself to the development of godly responses.

I understand that this includes my commitment to a right attitude and actions based on God's Word.

Signed: _____

Dated: _____

"The Lord is my strength and my shield; my heart trusted in Him, and I am helped; therefore my heart greatly rejoices, and with my song I will praise Him."
(Psalm 28:7)

GLOSSARY

GLOSSARY

adaptability - the ability to adapt, to change to meet expectations, to be flexible, to adjust to new circumstances. (22)

allegation - a statement charging a wrongdoing without it being proved. (31)

anger - an emotional response to not obtaining what was desired; can be destructive when it harms the person or harms others. (20) (21)

anoint - to place oil on a chosen person's head to indicate a special service he is to perform. (33)

aptitude - having a natural ability or talent for certain work. (33)

attitude - the mental or emotional mindset that is shown in outward behaviors. Having a positive attitude is critical to success. (33)

avarice - extreme desire for getting money. (30)

background - family position, finances, skills, talents, etc., which a person has, or doesn't have, which can lead to a sense of self-concept. (28)

blame - to charge another person with wrongdoing. (31) (32)

capable - being able to accomplish what is desired, having abilities. (28)

carnal - related to the flesh, having a focus on the world's pleasure. (32)

celebration - a joyous marking of a special occasion. (32)

challenge - to face a problem or difficulty that needs to be solved. (26)

choice - to choose between options, to determine or direct by personal will. (32)

compare - to consider the value of things in relation to each other. (25)

competency - ability to perform at a satisfactory level. (25)

concupiscence - the desire for more and more, never being satisfied with life, living in excess. (30)

consequence - the result of a decision or action, a related reaction or outcome. (26)

GLOSSARY

contentment - a peace and satisfaction that occurs when you accept who you are and what God has given you. (28)

courageous - having courage or strength to do right even though facing great challenges or dangers. (28)

covenant - a binding, unbreakable promise that describes an agreement or relationship between two or more individuals. (29)

covetousness - an uncontrolled desire to have the things that belong to others, materialism. (30)

criticism - corrective, constructive words meant to help a person. Criticism can be negative when it involves ridicule and scorn. (29) (31) (32)

deception - causing others to accept as true that which is false. It includes lies, untruths, half-truths, falsehoods, exaggerations and spins. (23)

depression - a mental and emotional state in which a person is sad, has no energy or interest in life, etc., that is intense and lasts more than two weeks. (34)

desires - the wants and dreams a person has. (30)

despair - to lose all hope, to feel that everything is lost, to want to give up and not try. (34)

disappointment - feeling sad or bitter that you did not get or achieve what you wanted. (30)

discontent - to have an absence of peace and satisfaction; a feeling of being unhappy with what you have or who you are. (30)

discouragement - a mental and emotional state of being sad, disheartened, unenthusiastic. It is less severe than depression and usually goes away in less than two weeks. (34)

double portion - an ancient tradition in which the eldest son inherited twice the amount of other brothers. It was a sign of family leadership and blessing from the father. It made the eldest son responsible for the care of unmarried sisters and parents. (26)

duration - a measure of time, how long something lasts. (34)

GLOSSARY

eternal - without time limits, ever-lasting, future that will never end. (32)

evil - sinful, wrong, opposite to good and right; describes activities opposed to God and promoted by Satan. (26)

exile - living in another country because of being removed from your own country, usually as a captive or slave. (27)

faith - a strong belief that what God says is absolutely true; to act in confidence on that belief. (26) (29)

faithful - demonstrating faith, loyal, regular in habit, dependable, able to be counted on. (35)

false accusations - charges made against a person that are untrue or half true. (31)

falsehood - an untruth or lie. (23)

flexibility - the ability to be flexible, to bend and not break, to easily change directions in order to get along with others. (22)

friend - a person, other than family, with whom you enjoy a positive relationship. (27)

fury - excessive anger. (20)

godliness/godly - a sincere desire and effort to live according to the principles of God's Word. (28) (31)

great gain - true wealth or riches—treasures in Heaven. (28)

habits - repeated behaviors that become automatic; actions done without thinking. (23)

half-truth - a whole lie that has some partial truth in it. (23)

humble - being meek, recognizing one's position in relationship to God, considering self less often than the good of others. (28) (35)

hypocrite - someone who says one thing but does another, acting different from what the person really is on the inside. (21)

inadequacies - the root of the word is unequal; it is the sense that our abilities are limited, we are insufficient for the task, we don't measure up, we are unable to satisfy the requirements, feelings of inferiority, insecurity, incompetence, poor self-concept, low self-esteem. (25)

GLOSSARY

inferiority - being less than satisfactory; a sense a person has that he is less than adequate. (25)

insurmountable - not able to be overcome, involves too great a risk or too great a potential for defeat. (24)

integrity - all parts are complete (whole) and fit together in perfect unity; to walk with integrity is to walk in truth. (23)

intensity - a measure of strength, how often or how severely something occurs. (34)

impossible - not possible, not doable, not achievable. (24)

isolation - being set apart or cut off from the group, being alone. (27)

irony - an unexpected outcome, an odd occurrence, parts that don't add up. (25)

joy - a feeling of deep happiness and satisfaction; rejoicing. (32)

judge - to evaluate, to determine the truth, to express judgment such as in criticism. (32)

lasciviousness - sensual, lewd; living without self-control. (30)

lies - untrue statements with the intent to deceive. (23) (31)

life changes - the challenges a person must face in life that require a difference in the way he responds or feels. Some life changes are expected, others are unanticipated and cause disruption to our lives. (22)

loneliness - feeling alone, without friends; feeling sad because you don't have someone to share with. (27)

love - deep affection and caring for another. (27)

materialism - the drive to obtain more and better possessions. (19)

ministry - work done as a service to God or mankind. (35)

mocking - making fun of or ridicule in a harmful manner. (29)

motive - an internal need or desire that causes someone to act a certain way. (21) (32)

GLOSSARY

obedience - the act of obeying, to follow directions, to do what an authority orders. (24) (33)

obstacle - a block or hindrance to getting or accomplishing what you desire. (33)

occupation - job, vocation, what one does to earn money. (35)

offer - to give, to extend for another person's use. Deborah willingly offered herself to God. (24)

omnipotence - all powerful; an attribute of God that means He has complete authority and control over all things, including the things that happen to us. (22)

omniscience - all knowing; an attribute of God that means He knows all things past, present and future; therefore, He is never caught unaware or surprised by anything. (22)

opportunities - favorable times or places for you to achieve something; chances. (33)

overwhelming - overpowering, so great as to dishearten or cause fear. (24)

persecution - the acts of ridicule and vengeance which are meant to discourage or harm a person. (29)

persevere - to continue through a struggle, to last, to hold on or to stand during difficult times. (29)

pervert - to change by twisting or wringing; perversion is lying or a twisting of the truth. (23)

position - a place or pose; a place in life that provides status, pride and power. (19)

possessions - things we obtain and collect that can cause pride. (19)

possible - able to be done, achievable, certain of accomplishment. (24)

poverty - being poor, having insufficient money to secure the basic necessities of life. (28)

praise - to express thanks and adoration to someone. God especially desires the praises of His children. (34)

presumptuous - being prideful, focused only on self; to assume that you are more important or better than others.(26)

GLOSSARY

pretender - a person who pretends to be something he is not; an actor; a person who lives a lie. (25)

pride - a sense of self-importance, to assume a position above others of equal status, to think you must be first and best. (26)

priest - a server in the Temple of God from the tribe of Levi. Only the High Priest could offer annual sacrifices in the Holy of Holies. (33)

principle - a basic belief about what is important or how things work. (26)

priorities - beliefs or actions that have prime importance in life; what must be done first or above all others. (32)

prophet - a person who spoke God's message, sometimes as in foretelling future events, but more often in forth-telling warnings to repent. (33)

providence - the oversight, care and direction of God in our lives. (19)

pure in heart - sincere; having honest motives. Jesus said, "Blessed are the pure in heart." (21)

rage - anger that has swirled out of control and is likely to erupt into negative reactions. (20)

realistic - having qualities that give the appearance of being real. Realistic goals are possible and achievable. (24)

reasons - causes; explanations of why a person acted a certain way. (21)

regret - to be sorry for an action. (30)

religious - having religion or belief in powers higher than one's self; following a set of laws or expectations based on a religion. A person can be religious but not be a godly Christian. (31)

repentance - changing directions; to be sorry for and turn from sin. (21)

reprove - to rebuke, scold, criticize. (32)

resilience - the ability to rebound after experiencing difficult challenges in life. (22)

GLOSSARY

revenge - the effort to get even or retaliate against someone for some perceived wrong. (20) (21)

ridicule - to use hurtful, sarcastic words to make fun of, to tear down and harm emotionally. (29)

sacred - related to holy things dedicated to God's use; opposite to secular. (35)

sarcasm - words said in a cutting, hurtful way. (29)

secular - related to human everyday life; opposite to sacred. (35)

security - safety, confidence; without doubt, distrust or fear. (23)

self-centered - to be selfish, focused only on self interests or needs. (32)

self-concept - the opinions and beliefs a person has about himself; related to self-esteem which is the value a person perceives of himself. (25) (28)

selfish - concerned only for self interests and needs without care for others' feelings or benefit. (32)

service - activity done to benefit another person. (35)

slander - words meant to tear down and hurt another person. (31)

solitary - lonely, secluded or remote from others. (27)

soul - the eternal part of a person that responds to God; spirit. (19)

sovereignty of God - the unlimited power God has to control the affairs of nature and history. (19) (26)

stand for - to be in favor of; to support as in standing for the cause of Christ. (29)

status - a place or position that brings honor and respect from others. (19)

steward - a person placed in a position to responsibly manage the property of another. (35)

stewardship - wise, responsible management of the things entrusted to us, including abilities and possessions. (19) (35)

GLOSSARY

success - attaining or achieving your goals. Success with God is to be obedient and conformed to His image. (33)

suffering - experiencing difficult problems, calamities, disasters, etc., over which a person has little control; enduring emotional or physical pain. (26)

sufficiency - the amount needed or expected, adequacy, competence, ability to perform. (25)

survive - to live through a difficult experience or a life-threatening situation. (I)

temporal - related to time; opposite to eternal. (32)

temptation - an enticement or invitation to sin, with the implied promise of good to be gained from following the path of disobedience. (20) (31)

thrive - to overcome challenges in a way that you are more successful than ever before. (I)

tragedy - a traumatic, terrible event such as an unexpected death in a family, diagnosis of a terminal illness, etc., that produces great emotional pain. (26)

transition - changing from one situation or place to another. (22)

trust - to believe, to have faith, to totally depend on someone, to have a sure confidence. (23) (26)

truth - being honest, factual, without error or deception. God's nature is truth and He expects us to be truth-tellers. (23)

unfulfilled dreams - goals and desires in life that a person would hope to achieve but doesn't, or if achieved never satisfy. (30)

unrealistic expectations - goals or behaviors imposed by others, or self, that seem to be beyond our ability and are therefore impossible to accomplish. (24)

value - to hold in esteem, to consider worthy or important. (28)

vengeance - the act of taking revenge, to get even, to strike back in order to hurt a person for a wrong done to you. (29)

GLOSSARY

violence - the physical damage to people or property that results from expressed anger. (20)

vocation - a chosen field of work, occupation or ministry. (35)

wealth - money or possessions that have high value, riches. (19) (28)

willingly - done without pressure or force, freely giving oneself or possessions to be used for a purpose. (24)

worthy - valuable, important. People are deemed worthy because they are created in God's image; Christians are deemed worthy because they are new creations in Christ Jesus. (28)

wrath - anger directed toward individuals; fury. (20)

YHWH - the holiest name of God meaning I AM WHO I AM; it conveys God's eternal self-existence. (25)

Prescriptions
for
Life Challenges

PRESCRIPTIONS FOR LIFE'S CHALLENGES

Surviving and Thriving
Romans 8:18, 28, 31b, 35, 37
Jeremiah 31:3 and 29:11

Bad Things That Happen
Job 19:25 and 27
Job 13:15
Psalm 61:11–12
2 Timothy 2:12
2 Timothy 3:12
Hebrews 11:25
1 Peter 3:14

Challenges of Service
1 Corinthians 4:1–2
1 Peter 4:10–11
Matthew 20:26–28
Titus 3:8, 14

Critical Spirit
Psalm 100
Psalm 27:4–5
Psalm 141:5
Proverbs 27:9
Colossians 4:5–6
Luke 6:31, 36–37, 41–42
James 4:11–12

Destructive Anger
Ephesians 4:26–27
Ephesians 4:31–32
James 1:19–20
Psalm 103:8
Proverbs 15:1
Colossians 3:8

Discouragement
Romans 15:5–6
John 14:27; 16:33
Proverbs 3:26
Psalm 37:3
Psalm 30:5, 11
2 Corinthians 4:8–9, 16–18
Revelation 21:3–4

False Accusations
Romans 12:17–19
Daniel 10:12
Proverbs 16:7
Psalm 31:23–24
Daniel 1:8
Matthew 5:43–44

Habits of Deception
Psalm 34:12–14
(1 Peter 3:10–11)
Proverbs 10:9
Galatians 6:7
Ephesians 4:25, 29
Proverbs 8:6–8
Proverbs 12:15; 20:17
Colossians 2:8–10

Life Changes
Philippians 4:12–13
Psalm 121
Psalm 139:1–18
Acts 16:31–32; 20:20–21

Loneliness
1 John 4:21–5:2
Psalm 16:7–9
Psalm 37:25–28
John 14:23–27
Deuteronomy 13:6–8

Obstacles to Success
1 Samuel 15:22
1 John 2:3–4
James 1:22, 25
Deuteronomy 30:14, 19
Psalm 27:13–14
Ephesians 6:6–7

Personal Inadequacies
2 Corinthians 3:4–5
Ephesians 2:10
Psalm 28:7
Philippians 1:6; 2:13
Ephesians 3:16–17
Ephesians 4:23
2 Corinthians 12:9–10
1 Corinthians 1:25–26

Poor Background
Jeremiah 29:11–13
2 Corinthians 5:17
2 Corinthians 3:17–18
Matthew 10:29–31
Judges 2:12, 16, 18
1 Timothy 6:6–7

Ridicule and Vengeance
Matthew 5:10–12
Ephesians 4:31–32
Galatians 5:13–15
1 Peter 3:8–12
1 Peter 4:12–16, 19
Genesis 7:1, 5, 23
Hebrews 11:6–7

Position and Possessions
Mark 8:35–37
1 Timothy 6:8–10
Matthew 6:21, 24, 33
Philippians 4:11–13
Matthew 25:21
Proverbs 11:4

Unfulfilled Dreams
Ecclesiastes 12:1a, 13–14
Colossians 3:1–3
Psalm 20:4; 40:8; 37:4
Matthew 6:29–33
Luke 12:16, 22–31
1 Chronicles 28:9
2 Chronicles 1:11–12

Unrealistic Expectations
Matthew 11:28–30
Philippians 4:13, 19
Psalm 20:4–5
1 Samuel 17:47
2 Samuel 22:7
Psalm 18:1–3
Psalm 22:3–5
Psalm 36:5–9

Wrong Motives
Proverbs 16:2–3
Matthew 15:18–19
Philippians 4:8
Proverbs 23:7
Psalm 15

NOTES